AF255919

Charles Edward Davis, D.D.

A Servant's Life: The Chronology

"Tomorrow is Today"

Dr. Thelma Manning Hall, Ph. D.
WITH Charles Edward Davis, D.D.
author of the More Than a Conqueror series

Charles Edward Davis, D.D.

A Servant's Life: The Chronology

ISBN: 978-1-948638-48-7 (hardcover)

Unless otherwise indicated, all Scripture quotations are taken from the King James Version of the Bible.

Published by

Fideli Publishing, Inc.
119 W. Morgan St.
Martinsville, IN 46151

www.FideliPublishing.com

PRINTED IN THE UNITED STATES OF AMERICA

Dedication

This book is dedicated to the Charles Edward Davis family, his dear friends and all the members of the Indiana Avenue Pentecostal Church of God, Inc. (past and present); All the Churches and Pastors of the Illinois District Council; Wyoming Council, Pacific Northwest District Council and the New York and Ontario Council; The Board of Bishops of the Pentecostal Assemblies of the World, Inc; The Chicago Business Community; the political community of the United States Senate, United States House of Representative, Office of the Governor, State of Illinois:State Senators, State Representatives, Assemblyman, Alderman and Office of the Mayor; Office of Circuit Court of Cook County, Office of Cook County Assessor; Office of the Recorder of Deeds; Office of Cook County Board of Review; and Office of Cook County Commissioners

Acknowledgements

This book is the joint compilation of staff and members of the Indiana Avenue Pentecostal Church of God, Incorporation. In making this book possible, special acknowledgements for contributions received from:

Mr. Otis Buckley, Photographer and member, Indiana Avenue Pentecostal Church of God, Inc., Chicago, Illinois.

Mrs. Katie Walker-Buckley, Executive Administrator to Bishop Charles E. Davis, and member, Indiana Avenue Pentecostal Church of God, Inc., Chicago, Illinois.

Dr. Joyce Walker, Member, Indiana Avenue Pentecostal Church of God Ministerial Alliance, Chicago, Illinois.

Pictures in Book: 1st Book of Davis, Author: Evangelist Joyce Washington-Walker.

Dr. Margaret Wright, member of the Board of Directors, Indiana Avenue Pentecostal Church of God, Inc., Chicago, Illinois.

Dr. Thelma Manning Hall, former youth secretary to Bishop Charles Edward Davis and later elevated to church secretary to Elder Odee Akines, Pastor of the Indiana Avenue Pentecostal Church of God, Inc., Chicago, Illinois. Dr. Hall served in various positions at the national levels of Pentecostal Assembles of the World, Inc., with Bishop Charles Edward Davis and Mrs. Geraldine Olivia Davis.

Special thanks to Robin Surface, publisher, for her exceptional talent and outstanding service. Without her, this book could not have been completed.

Table of Contents

The Legacy: Charles Edward Davis

May the intent of this book inspire all Christians to be a better you in Christ and a super conqueror for Christ.

To define a spiritual servant is one who volunteers of their time, talent and treasure to be used to further the causes of the kingdom of God.

A spiritual servant lives a Christ centered life that demonstrates loyalty to God; dedication to the work of the Lord; seeks to please God according to the Word of the Lord; seeks to develop oneself spiritually; and help others develop spiritually; makes sacrifices for the work of the Lord; and is ever learning to exhort the word of the Lord.

Charles Edward Davis has lived ninety-six years on this earth. In nine decades of his life, he has seen many changes. After he dedicated his life to Christ, he became focused, steadfast and unmovable in the work of the Lord. When said another way, each quarter of his life he has demonstrated a belief, a thirst and a hunger for excelling in the work of the Lord.

In the **first quarter** of his life, he attended school, graduated and served his country honorably.

In the **second quarter** of his life, he did not know God. God led him from the clubs and lounges into the house of the Lord. Many good developments happened thereafter.

In the **third quarter** of his life, it was in the Church that he found the true calling and purpose for his life's work.

In the **fourth quarter** of his life, he has encouraged the young adults and the seniors to pursue higher education; to serve God; to live a godly life; to read your Bible and exercise your faith in God and to perform in a spirit of excellence.

The Indiana Avenue Pentecostal Church of God, Incorporated is the one true passion of Charles Edward Davis. He has pursued and achieved a great legacy.

Preface

Bishop Charles Edward Davis has served as pastor of the Indiana Avenue Pentecostal Church of God, Incorporated, Chicago, Illinois from 1970 to present. He is a man of commitment, integrity, faith, fortitude, a visionary, trailblazer, builder, administrator, spiritual counselor, strong community supporter and a friend to thousands.

He is an ambassador and a true conqueror for God. His love for God and his love for people can be witnessed in the many lives that his life has inspired. He is a man of exemplary character and stands firm on what he believes. He continues to set a high standard of excellence for the body of Christ.

Charles Edward Davis is dedicated to helping humanity, whether members of his church or people of the community. He is highly respected among religious and secular leaders within the community.

His academic and secular accomplishments are many and he has received countless letters of commendation, plaques, and accolades from religious, political and community organizations.

As recorded in Luke 2:52, "And Jesus increased in wisdom and stature, and in favor with God and man." This is one of the many scriptures Bishop Davis has embraced, but there are many scriptures that has demonstrated his successful walk with God. He found favor with God and with man and continues to increase in wisdom.

He is a husband, a father, a grandfather, a great-grandfather and a lover of God's people.

Charles Edward Davis, D.D.

Life Cycle in Quarters

FIRST **25 YEARS** 1923–1948 25 years of age	**SECOND** **25 YEARS** 1949–1974 50 years of age
THIRD **25 YEARS** 1975–2000 75 years of age	**FOURTH** **25 YEARS** 2001–2019 76–96 years of age

CHAPTER 1

Childhood

Charles Edward Davis was born in Leland, Mississippi on October 2, 1923 to Priscilla Hobbs. His birth name was Walter Lewis, but not for long. His mother changed his name to Charles Edward Davis. He had one brother, William Mc Kinley Davis.

At the age of 4, in 1927, there was a flood in Leland, Mississippi and the family moved to Chicago, Illinois. Two years later, at the age of 6, the family experienced and survived the great depression.

In 1940, at age 17, his family moved a second time to Chicago, Illinois and lived in the Bronzeville neighborhood.

As a child, he was taught to save a portion of his money. It was instilled in him that pennies made dollars. With his savings, he bought a zoot suit. Later, he learned that the zoot suit was no longer in style and he decided that he would not follow the style, but would purchase conservative clothes.

CHAPTER 2

Education

In 1929, Charles Edward Davis lived in the Bronzeville neighborhood in Chicago, where he received his education. The legal age for children to start school was five years old. He started at age six, which put him a year behind his peers.

This did not stop him from pursuing his education. He graduated high school in 1937. He wanted to become a math teacher, but instead he entered the military. He took his math books with him to the military, but was unable to fulfill his dream of becoming a math teacher.

CHAPTER 3

Military

In 1942, at age 19, Charles Edward Davis served his country in the United States Army at Fort Francis Warren Air Force Base. He did his boot camp training in Cheyenne, Wyoming.

His tour of duty allowed him to serve his country in France, Holland, and Germany. He received an honorable discharge. His exit date was January 10, 1946.

He received two medals that were pinned to his chest 64 years later on his 86th birthday. Dr. Joyce Walker was able to obtain his World War II medals, which he had left behind when his tour of duty was over. Dr. Joyce Walker also published his story in the magazine titled *3:16*.

In 1946, Charles Edward Davis pursed his education for upholstery and made Elder Charles Haywood Ellis a hasset.

The years 1947–1953 represent his life before "the change" to live for Jesus.

CHAPTER 4

HISTORICAL INFORMATION

Elder Charles Haywood Ellis, Founder The Indiana Avenue Pentecostal Church of God, Inc.

(1934–1953)

Elder Charles Haywood Ellis was born April 29, 1900 to Reverend and Mrs. William Ellis in Musgooga County, Georgia, near Columbus, Georgia. He was united in Holy matrimony in November 1918 to Miss Florence Lucille Rucker. He moved to Chicago in 1920 with their two children. By 1942, there were eleven children added to the family.

He had very little education, but was blessed by God to be able to cope with all types of people. He made many, many friends and was loved by all who knew him.

He put church work before everything. He loved the church and the members. He did not want to tear up the church and did not want anyone to destroy the church.

He encouraged the saints to love one another as a big family.

Elder Charles Haywood Ellis was a member of the Freewill Church of God. As doctrinal dialog was exchanged, there was a division. Elder Ellis was a firm faith believer. He trusted God. He accepted the Bible as truth. After leaving the Freewill Church of God, Elder Ellis accepted the election of the saints and became their pastor in October of 1934.

The new church was located at 3455 South Prairie Avenue, to a building which was in poor condition. For two years it was called "Church." Later the church was renamed, "The Pentecostal Church of God."

Elder Ellis struggled in many ways to build a house for God. On Sunday and Tuesday nights, he would line up chairs on the sidewalk. Saints enjoyed singing the songs of Zion using rub boards, drums, cymbals, tambourines, horns and guitars. Ministers would preach from the Word of God and souls were added to the church.

After attending the General Convention of the Pentecostal Assemblies of the World, in Detroit, Michigan, his church was nominated to become a member of the Pentecostal Assemblies of the World, Inc. In 1939, he became an official member of the Pentecostal Assemblies of the World, Inc., an international Interracial organization, headquartered in Indianapolis, Indiana. The Indiana Avenue Pentecostal Church of God, Inc has remained a member of the Pentecostal Assemblies of the World, Inc. for 80 years.

In April 1941, the church moved to its new church home, 3522 South Indiana Avenue, Chicago, Illinois. This property was dedicated to the Lord by District Elder J. S. Holly. In 1943, just 18 months later, the church purchased the vacant lot next door to the church at 3520 South Indiana Avenue. In 1945 a used motor bus was purchased and converted into a dining room and dinners were served and funds were used for the church.

The annual church convention started the fourth Sunday in October and continued for two weeks. As souls gave their lives to Christ at the revivals, the candidates for baptism was taken to the Apostolic Faith Church at 3813 Indiana Avenue, Chicago, Illinois, pastored by District Elder John S. Holly.

Elder Ellis envisioned a large Sunday School. The Sunday School enrollment grew to 150 members. He was blessed to see his vision fulfilled before his demise in 1953.

CHAPTER 5

ADDITIONAL HISTORICAL INFORMATION

Elder Odee Akines, Second Pastor The Indiana Avenue Pentecostal Church of God, Inc.

(1954–1970)

Elder Odee Akines was born March 18, 1902 to Reverend James and Emma Akines in Rosedale, Mississippi. He was united in Holy matrimony to Miss Rosie O'Neal on October 1, 1938. To this union was born two sons, Benjamin and Odee, Jr. He came to Chicago, Illinois in 1922.

He became a member of the Indiana Avenue Pentecostal Church of God, Inc. on August 23, 1941 which was four months after Elder Ellis had moved into the new edifice at 3522 South Indiana Avenue.

Five years later, in December 1946, he became a minister.

The death of our founder, the late Elder Charles Haywood Ellis, occurred in 1953. A year later, on April 15, 1954, the church members elected Elder Odee Akines as Pastor of the Indiana Avenue Pentecostal Church of God, Inc.

Elder Akines was a meek and gentle man. His wife, Rosie Akines, was faithful and served with her husband and was given to hospitality. Of their two sons, one son, Ben Akines, worked diligently in the church.

Elder Akines preached the word of God and taught the saints to be faithful. He encouraged the young people to stay active in the church and appointed Brother Charles Edward Davis to keep the young people busy. He also informed Brother Charles Edward Davis that he would have to get himself another secretary because he was elevating his secretary, Sister Thelma Manning, to be the church secretary.

Elder Akines remained as pastor of the Indiana Avenue Pentecostal Church of God, Inc. for 16 years, from 1954 until his demise in 1970.

CHAPTER 6

Religious Experience (1954) The Amazing Saving Grace of God

LIFE AFTER THE CHANGE TO LIVE FOR CHRIST

Before becoming a member of the church, Charles Edward Davis met Elder Charles Haywood Ellis, Pastor and founder of the Indiana Avenue Pentecostal Church of God, Inc. He had no intention of becoming a member, but one of the church mothers began to reason with him.

It was Mother Anastasia Anderson who witnessed to him about the saving grace of God, and he accepted the Lord Jesus as his personal Savior. Charles Edward Davis was baptized in Jesus name, and received the Holy Ghost according to Acts 2:38.

He became a member of the Indiana Avenue Pentecostal Church of God on May 7, 1954.

His life was no longer his own. He became a dedicated servant for the Lord Jesus Christ. He often mentions, he is thankful that God delivered him from his old lifestyle and instead of walking into the clubs, and lounges, he was now walking into God's house.

CHAPTER 7

Marriage to Geraldine Olivia Bush

(1954–1998)

Charles Edward Davis was married to Geraldine Olivia Bush for 43 Years.

During his marriage to Sister Geraldine Olivia Davis, Charles Edward Davis had her full support. She encouraged him to be active in the church ministry and she served by his side until she went to be with the Lord, September, 1998.

Sister Geraldine Olivia Davis embraced Sister Thelma Manning as their other daughter and asked her to provide secretarial services for their church positions at local, state and national levels.

In 1955, he was appointed to the position of youth leader. Under his leadership, he was able to keep the young people busy.

He organized both the Junior Usher Board and the Vacation Bible School, with 125 students in attendance.

He was appointed superintendent of the Sunday School.

He was also appointed the chairman of the Indiana Avenue Pentecostal Church Choir.

Later, he was appointed Finance Committee Chairman and his Secretary would prepare the deposit slips and would record all financial transactions.

While married to Sister Geraldine Olivia Davis, he was able to grow spiritually and secularly. His spiritual and academic achievements were never-ending. The more he learned the more he wanted to learn. At 95 years of age, after you read his accomplishments, you will agree, he is a life-long learner.

CHAPTER 8

Academic Achievement

(1960–1993)

Academics

Six years into his marriage, he earned an Associate of Arts Degree from Stanton University,1960

Six years later he earned a Bachelor of Liberal Arts Degree from Bradford University, 1966

Eight years after that, he earned a Parliamentary Procedures Certificate, Central YMCA College, 1974

Two years later, he earned a Bachelor of Bible Theology, Universal Bible Institute, 1976

He also earned a Preliminary Teachers Certificate, Evangelical Teacher Training Association (ETTA).

Advanced Education (1979–1993)

Master of Bible Theology Degree, Southern Bible Seminary, 1979

Doctor of Divinity, Honorary Degree, Aenon Bible College, 1986

Doctor of Theology Degree, Pentecostal Bible College, 1989

Doctor of Humanities, Theology and Philosophy, and Church Administration, International Apostolic University of Grace and Truth, 1993

CHAPTER 9

Servant/Leader
The Leadership of Chief

Under the leadership of Elder Odee Akines, Brother Charles Davis was asked to serve as president of the IPC Senior Choir (1955). It was during this time, he earned the title "Chief." The young people soon learned that his "No" was "No." He did not change his answer no matter how hard the young people might have tried to convince him.

As president of the young people's union, he used his car to take choir members home; some lived on the south side and some lived on the west side, and he took some home even as far as Monee, Illinois.

He insisted that the young people attend Monday night prayer meeting, Thursday night Bible Study and Saturday choir rehearsals. He accomplished many projects. One of his first purchases was a Leslie Speaker for the Hammond organ.

While firm, yet the softer gentle side of the Chief, Brother Davis would find young people jobs at Hart, Schaffer & Mark where he worked. If he recommended a young person, the personnel office was sure to hire his recommendation. Chief would counsel the young people to excel in every aspect of their life by pursuing their education.

Brother Charles Edward Davis was called to the ministry while serving as youth leader and preached his first sermon, "The Uncertainty of God."

It was later, he acknowledged to Pastor Akines that he wanted to pastor a church in Rockford, Illinois. He would drive to Rockford and return to Indiana Avenue Church of God, Inc (IPC) to carry out his duties as Finance Committee Chairman (1967) at the Indiana Avenue Pentecostal Church of God.

Elder Akines requested Minister Davis to return to Chicago and give up his quest of pastoring in Rockford. Pastor Akines further told Minister Davis he was needed more at his home church. Minister Davis gave up his desire to pastor in Rockford and returned to Indiana Avenue Pentecostal Church to fulfill his duties as Finance Chairman.

He supervised over-the-road trips on the church owned bus, "Old Betsy" to various States, such as, Indiana,

Michigan, Ohio, Pennsylvania, Wisconsin, Minnesota and Texas to name a few.

He served in the kitchen and was known for his golden-brown fried cat fish sandwiches, which were sold after church services and especially during revival services or during the Church Annual Conventions.

This activity provided the young people's department with finances to give the church and put funds in the young people's treasure for future activities.

Brother Charles Davis served as Sunday School Superintendent and implemented graded Sunday school literature for grades K through 12.

CHAPTER 10

HISTORICAL INFORMATION

Elder Charles Edward Davis, Third Pastor
The Indiana Avenue
Pentecostal Church of God, Inc.

Elder Charles Edward Davis was elected in 1970 by the congregation to be the pastor of the Indiana Avenue Pentecostal Church of God, Inc. He never had thoughts of becoming pastor of the church he avoided in the Bronzeville neighborhood where he lived and attended school.

After he was voted pastor of the Indiana Avenue Pentecostal Church, Inc., he resigned his job from Hart, Schaffner and Marx to become full-time pastor.

As full-time pastor, he was determined to give God the same amount of time from 8 a.m. am to 5 p.m. as he had given to previous employer, Hart, Schafner & Mark. In addition to his daily operations of the church, he was never too busy to visit and pray for the members of the congregation who were sick in the hospital, in the nursing homes or in hospice care.

- **2003** — The Education Department of the Indiana Avenue Pentecostal Church of God, Inc., presented a plaque of Congratulations to Bishop Charles Edward Davis for the conferred Doctorate of Humanities, Theology, Divinity, and Philosophy degrees. We are proud of you!

- **2003** — District Elder Allen and Sister Jacqueline Tate presented a plaque to, "Our Dynamic, Anointed, Visionary, Father, Bishop Charles Edward Davis."

- **2003** — Pastor was honored him with eloquent banquet for his 80th Birthday

- **2006** — The Indiana Avenue Pentecostal Church of God, Inc, Official Board awarded Bishop Charles Davis with a plaque to honor his 83rd Birthday.

- **2011** — The Sunday School Department, awarded the pastor with a crystal plaque, for 41 blessed years of service and leadership.

Down through the years, the Indiana Avenue Pentecostal Church of God, Inc. has shown their appreciation and love for their pastor and honored him with an eloquent banquet on his 90th Birthday (2013).

CHAPTER 11

Pastor/Builder/Visionary

(1984-1988)

As a pastor, builder and a visionary, he purchased surrounding properties and land in Chicago, Illinois, and there may be additional properties not named, but to name a few:

- 3 Lots on Michigan Avenue (3537, 3539, 3541)

- 3536 – 3546 South Indiana Avenue

- 4 Houses on Indiana Avenue (3601, 3517, 3532, 3534)

- 2 Church Buildings (3520-3522)

- 3 Houses (3525 through 3550)

- 117-133 East 35 Street & 3506 S. Indiana Avenue (Church Parking Lot)

- 114 – 122 East 36 Street

- 3 lots On Indiana Avenue (3515, 3525, 3528)

- 3 Houses — South Indiana Avenue (3611, 3613, 3635)

- Own the entire block West and East of 35th Street

- Owned and discontinued: A Print Shop and A funeral Home on Indiana Avenue

- 2 Lots on 57th State Street (5722, 5724)

In 2018, at the age of 95 years young, and as a visionary, Bishop Charles Edward Davis had thoughts, hopes and desires to build a senior housing facility titled Ellis-Akines-Davis Complex. Elder Charles Haywood Ellis, First Pastor; Elder Odee Akines, Second Pastor; and Bishop Charles Edward Davis, Third Pastor. This complex would give recognition to the founder and first pastor of the Indiana Avenue Pentecostal Church of God, Inc.

CHAPTER 12

Pentecostal Assemblies of the World, Inc. Illinois District Council Appointed to Elder (1970-1976)

Elder Charles Edward Davis became an ordained minister in 1970 recommended by the Diocesan Bishop John S. Holly of Chicago, Illinois and received his Ministerial Credential Certificate from the Pentecostal Assemblies of the World, Inc., Indianapolis, Indiana, USA.

Illinois District Council Positions (1970–1976)

While working in the council of church in the State of Illinois, as an Elder, Charles Edward Davis, served as council assistant chairman and was voted to become the council chairman. While holding the office of council chairman, he created auxiliaries and served as a council lay director. Order of positions are listed.

- Council Assistant Chairman

- Council Chairman

- Council Lay Director

- Organized and implemented a Ministerial Alliance

- Organized and implemented a Brotherhood Auxiliary

- Organized and implemented the Illinois Health Professionals*

He received a plaque which read:

"Honoring our Great Bishop & Leader, The Illinois District Council Health Professional of the PAW, Inc Wish to Honor Bishop Charles Edward Davis, Diocesan for your continued service to the Illinois District Council Health Professionals (IDCHP). We are sincerely grateful that you shared the vision God had in mind for us and commemorate you as one who we believe is meritorious. Thank you for demonstrating courage and great leadership."

- Elevated to District Elder

Pentecostal Assemblies of the World, Inc. Illinois District Council Appointed District Elder (1977–1986)

The Office of a District Elder shall have authority as delegated by the Bishop of the Diocese and may act in the Bishops absence. As an assistant to the Diocesan, Bishop J. S. Holly, Elder Charles Edward Davis was elevated to District Elder in the Illinois District Council. He was assigned to oversee seven churches and visit the churches within his district.

Four of the seven churches were namely: Grace Apostolic Church, Pastor, Cornelius Southern; One Way Apostolic Church, Pastor, Herman Walker; Christ Temple, Robin, IL Pastor Jackson; Dixmoor House of Prayer, Dixmoor, IL, Pastor Williams.

Elevated to Bishopric, Pentecostal Assemblies of the World, Inc, Headquarters, Indianapolis, Indiana. (1986)

Elevated to Diocesan Bishop
Pentecostal Assemblies of the World, Inc.

(1986–1988)

After having served the Illinois District Council as an elder for six years and a district elder for nine years, Charles Edward Davis was elevated to Bishop of the Pentecostal Assemblies of the World, Inc., Headquarters, Indianapolis, Indiana, he was assigned the following councils.

Assigned Diocesan Bishop of the Following Councils:

1. Wyoming Council, Pentecostal Assemblies of the World, Inc. (1986–1987)

2. Pacific Northwest Council, Pentecostal Assemblies of the World, Inc. (1987–1988)

NOTE: Received a plaque from the Pacific Northwest District Council presented to Bishop Charles Edward

David, D. D. "Appreciation as the new diocesan Bishop for the 17th Episcopal District of the PAW, Inc.

NOTE: New York State, Ontario & Canada, First Episcopal District of Pentecostal Assemblies of the World, Incorporated (1988–2007).

NOTE: The Diocesan Bishop Charles Edward Davis separated the one council aka New York Council from the Ontario & Canada Council.

3. New Council: New York District Council created by Bishop Charles Edward Davis.

4. New Council: Ontario & Canada created by Bishop Charles Edward Davis.

5. Elevated to Illinois, Six Episcopal District, Pentecostal Assemblies of the World, Inc. (July 1988–2013).

CHAPTER 15

Community Accomplishments

(1980 - 2019)

Bishop Charles Edward Davis generously provides opportunities for many young people to continue their secular and spiritual education through the following community outreach programs:

- Founder of God's Bible Institute

- The Bishop Charles E. Davis Scholarship

- Community Outreach Programs consist of:

- Clothing Giveaways

- Food donations

- Adopted a Pregnancy Women's Shelter

- Nursing Home Ministry

- Prison Ministry

- Back to School Annual Rally and school supplies give away

- Tutoring program

- GED program

- Black History Achievers Award*

A plaque for Black History Achievers Award was presented to Bishop Charles Davis from Judge Aleksandra Gillespie and Attorney Pat Heneghan which read:

"What You Have Demonstrated Within the African American Community is Considered "BEST IN CLASS." Your Contributions to The Upward Mobility of All Mankind Has Placed A Positive Light on The Future of Chicago. Your Labor Will Never Be in Vain."

CHAPTER 16

Affiliations

(1989 -1994)

- Ordained and Licensed Minister of the Pentecostal Assemblies of the World, Inc. (1970)

- Religious Conference Management Association (1989)

- Holman Health Board Facility (1991)

- Honored by the political community of Chicago who renamed the Indiana Avenue to Bishop Charles E. Davis Avenue (1992)

- Alternate Chaplain, City of Chicago Council

- Pastors Allied Under the Lord (PAUL)

- Who's Who Worldwide Registry of Global Business Leaders (1993—1994)

- Numerous Awards and Recognition received for Valor

CHAPTER 17

Marriage to Dr. Jessie Bell Kay

(2004 – 2019)

Bishop Charles Edward Davis married Dr. Jessie Bell Kay on November 28, 2004.

As of 2019, Dr. Jessie Bell Kay Davis has been married for 15 years to Bishop Charles Edward Davis. She has faithfully and diligently worked with her husband. She is always ready and willing to accompany him where ever his duties may lead him.

She has enjoyed making floral beautification arrangements for the sanctuary.

Dr. Jessie Bell Kay has held positions at local, state and national levels of the Pentecostal Assemblies of the World, Inc.

Dr. Jessie Bell Davis became advisor to the Women's Ministry and provided a name change: Called, Chosen, Faithful Women of Indiana Avenue Pentecostal Church of God, Inc.

Dr. Jessie Bell Davis has supported her husband and was present when Bishop Charles Edward Davis was awarded this plaque:

> The Episcopal Honor of Bishop Emeritus, presented to Bishop Charles Edward Davis, for thirty years of honorable and committed service to the mission and vision of the PAW, Inc., by the Presiding Prelate of the Pentecostal Assemblies of the World, Bishop Charles Haywood Ellis, III.

The Chronology of Recognition (1988–2016)

PHOTOS OF AWARDS / CERTIFICATES / PLAQUES

- Certificate: Bishop Charles Edward Davis, D.D., International Apostolic College of Grace and Truth, Doctorate of Divinity, 1993.

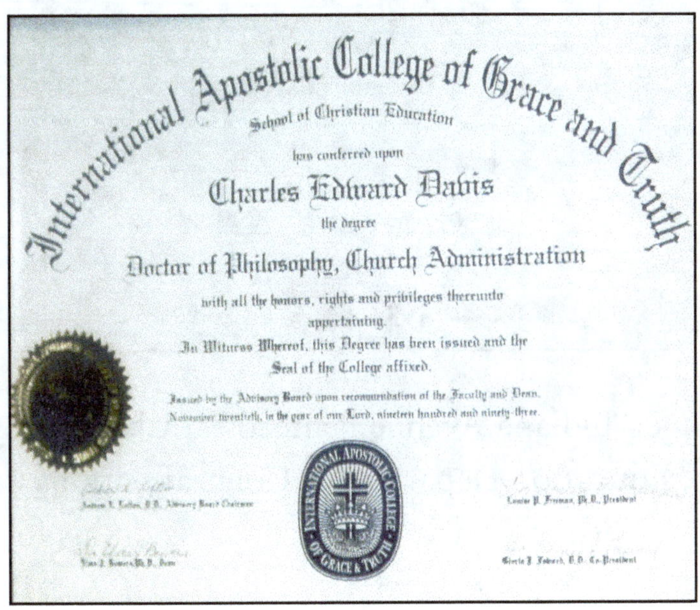

- Certificate: Bishop Charles Edward Davis, D.D., International Apostolic College of Grace and Truth, Doctorate of Philosophy, Church Administration, 1993.

- Certificate: Bishop Charles Edward Davis, D.D., International Apostolic College of Grace and Truth., Doctorate of Humanities, 1993.

- Certificate: Bishop Charles Edward Davis, D.D., Pentecostal Bible College, Doctorate of Theology, 2003.

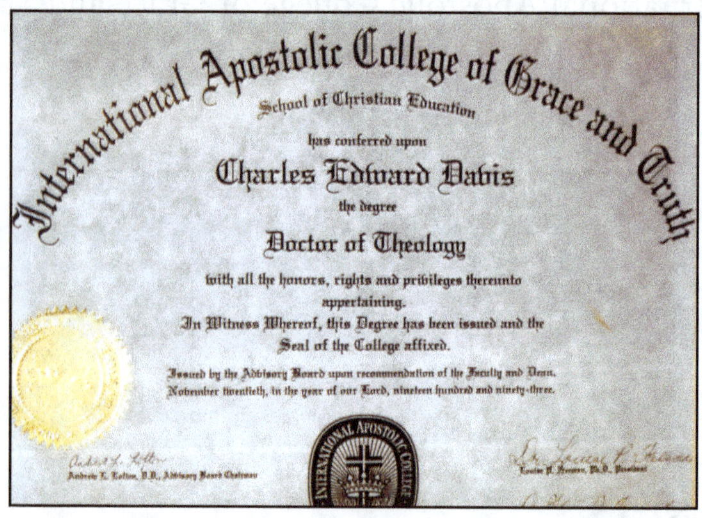

- Plaque: Indiana Avenue Pentecostal Church of God, Inc., Education Department, Congratulations to Pastor, Bishop Charles Edward Davis on his four doctorate degrees, 1993

• Plaque: Presented to Pastor Bishop Charles Edward Davis, D.D. of Indiana Avenue Pentecostal Church of God, Inc., 2003.

- Plaque: Presented to Pastor Bishop Charles Edward Davis, D.D., Indiana Avenue Pentecostal Church of God, Inc., 2006.

- Plaque: Indiana Avenue Pentecostal Church of God, Inc., Sunday School Department Award, Service and Leadership, Beloved Pastor Bishop Charles Edward Davis. D.D., 2011

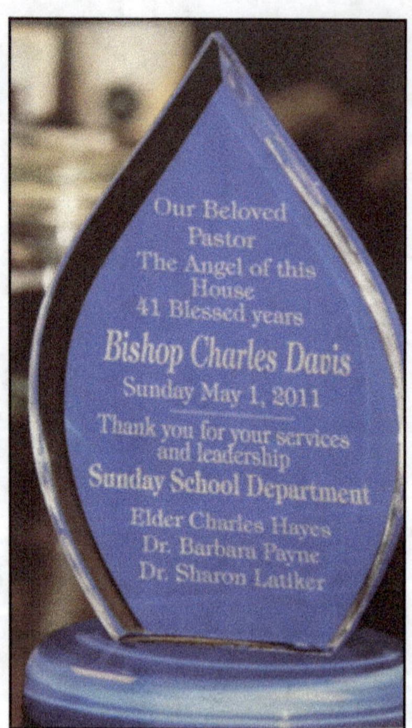

- The Indiana Avenue Pentecostal Church of God, Inc, Official Board awarded Bishop Charles Davis with a plaque to honor his 83rd Birthday.

- Certificate: Charles Edward Davis, Pentecostal Assemblies of the World, Inc., Headquarters, Indianapolis, Indiana, Ministerial Credential, 1970.

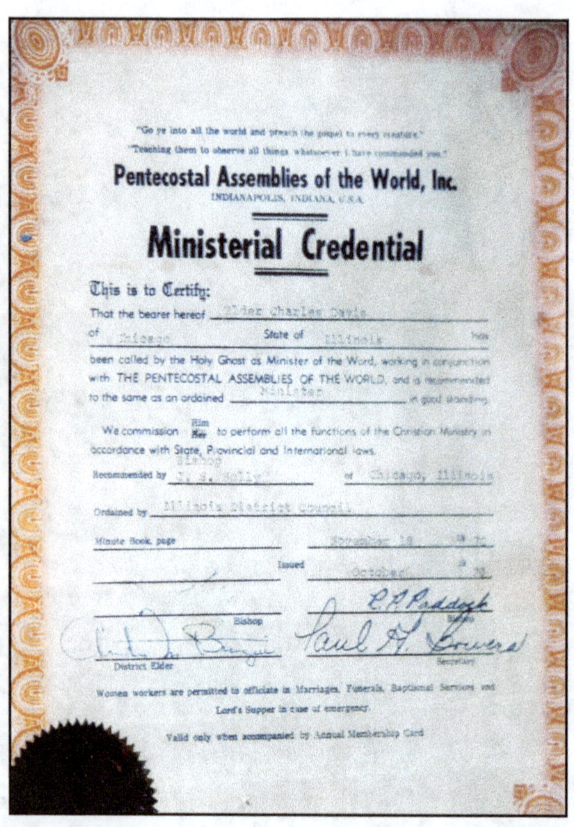

- Certificate: Bishop Charles Edward Davis, Pentecostal Assemblies of the World, Inc., Elevated to Bishop, 1986.

- Plaque: Bishop Charles Edward Davis, D.D., Pentecostal Assemblies of the World, Inc., Pacific Northwest Council, 1988.

- Plaque Award: Bishop Charles Edward Davis, D.D., Pentecostal Assemblies of the World, Inc., Convention Committee Chairman, 1999.

- Plaque: Presented to Bishop Charles Edward Davis, D. D., Pentecostal Assemblies of the World, Inc., Bishop Samuel L. Grimes Excellence Christian Ministry Award, 2016.

- Plaque: Bishop Charles Edward Davis was assigned by Pentecostal Assemblies of the World, Inc. as the diocesan of the Six Episcopal District, State of Illinois, Bishop Emeritus, 1984-2014. Presented by Bishop Charles Haywood Ellis, III, Presiding Prelate.

- Plaque: Presented to Bishop Charles Edward Davis, D. D., Joint Fellowship Service Pentecost Sunday, Illinois District Council of Pentecostal Assemblies of the World, Inc. (Paw) And Pentecostal Churches of the Apostolic Faith Chicago, Illinois, 2010.

- Plaque: Presented to Bishop Charles Edward Davis, D.D., Exemplary Leadership, Illinois District Council Ministers, Chicago, Illinois, 2013.

- Plaque: Presented to Bishop Charles Edward Davis, D. D., "Thank you for your leadership and friendship, from The Prince of Peace Apostolic Church, Chicago, Illinois, 2014.

- Plaque: Presented to Bishop Charles Edward Davis, D.D., Diocesan of New York & Ontario District Council, Salute for Outstanding Service and Leadership, 2001.

- Plaque: Presented to Diocesan Bishop Charles Edward Davis, D. D., New York & Ontario District Council, "Appreciate Your Spiritual Devotion and Your Leadership," 2001.

- Plaque: Bishop Charles Edward Davis, D.D., Diocesan of New York & Ontario District Council, Missionary & Christian Women's Auxiliary, 2003.

- Plaque: Presented to Bishop Charles Edward Davis, D.D., Who's Who Worldwide, Global Business Leader, 1993.

- Community Award: Presented to Bishop Charles Edward Davis, D.D., Political Recognition, Black History Achievers Award

CHAPTER 19

More Than a Conqueror

Six Powerful and Inspiring Messages

BY CHARLES EDWARD DAVIS, D.D.

Unless otherwise indicated, all Scripture quotations are taken from the King James Version of the Bible.

SIX POWERFUL INSPIRING LESSONS

Lesson 1 – Conquering Circumstances

Lesson 2 – Conquering Temptations

Lesson 3 – Conquering Fear

Lesson 4 – Conquering Discouragement

Lesson 5 – Conquering Inconsistencies

Lesson 6 – Conquering Worry

These lessons are geared toward making the saint of God an unbeatable champion in the fight against sin. I have been impressed by the Lord to speak on conquering" for a few weeks. I thought about it and I am going to share with you some of the areas you will need to conquer before you can become a "super conqueror."

SUPER CONQUEROR

Conquering Circumstances

For clarity, in the book of Genesis Chapter 6:1-8, I want you to reflect on God's goodness to you as we read these verses together.

The Flood, Genesis 6:1-8:

(1) *The marriage of Cainites with Sethites*

Verse 1: *And it came to pass when men began to multiply on the face of the earth and daughters were born unto them,*

Verse 2: *That the sons of God saw the daughters of men that they were fair; and took them wives of all whom they chose.*

(2) *The warning of Jehovah*

Verse 3: *And the Lord said, My spirit shall not always strive with man, for that he also is flesh: yet his days shall be 120 years.*

(3) The antediluvian civilization, Luke 17:27

Verse 4: *There were giants in the earth in those days; and also after that, when the sons of God came in unto the daughters of men, and they bare children to them, the same became mighty men which were of old, men of renown.*

(4) The purpose of Jehovah in judgment.

Verse 5: *And God saw that the wickedness of man was great in the earth, and they every imagination of the thoughts of his heart was only evil continually.*

Verse 6: *And it repented the Lord that he had made man on the earth, and it grieved him at his heart.*

Verse 7: *And the Lord said, I will destroy man whom I have created from the face of the earth; both man, and beast, and the creeping thing, and the fowls of the air; for it repenteth me that I have made them.*

Verse 8: *But Noah found grace in the eyes of the Lord.*

But Noah found grace in the eyes of the Lord. But Noah found grace in the eyes of the Lord. I want to speak on the subject, "Conquering your Circumstances."

If you are going to be a conqueror, you have got to be able to conquer while in your circumstances. If you are to become a super conqueror, you have got to be a conquer in every circumstance. You have to be a conqueror in everything; not just a few things but in everything.

There are times when most people and saints of God are spiritually tired, worn out, feel that many problems at home, at work, in the church, the government are too great for them to make realistic impact or try to correct their problems. We feel that nothing can be done, so we set back and accept things as they are. We say, "There is nothing I can do." So, we just accept life's circumstances and we are just willing to exist. As children of God, I believe that we ought to be found trying to find victory in the midst of our circumstances. We ought to be able to conquer them as a child of God.

When the Bible speaks of victory, triumphs and conquest, it means little more than foolishness to some, but these words are not a fantasy nor a foolish dream. You say, but you do not know what I am going through and you don't know my circumstances. I say, "I am glad I know a God who knows what we are going through and He knows your circumstances." Many times, you may not hear what the word of God is saying concerning the teaching of "victory." You hear me, as a preacher says, "victory." Brothers and sisters, you can have victory on your job, in your home, in your church or wherever you reside when you have a desire deep down in your soul to be a conquer and fight some battles to get the victory.

When I was in the Army, I saw infantry men wearing battle stars and I had no stars. I did not have as much time in the military as they had. I wanted to know why I did not have a star. It was said, "You haven't found any battles yet."

When you fight some battles, you get some victories, then you get some stars.

When you think about biblical personalities, Noah is the known character in the old testament to demonstrate conquering in your circumstances. So, I want to use Noah today because I think Noah can depict the subject of conquering your circumstances.

Noah's name is associated with one of the greatest catastrophes in the history of the human race. Noah was identified with the flood and in the midst of his trying circumstances, he was able to conqueror. From his conquest, from his victory, and from his triumphs, we can learn how to follow in truth and obedience in order to conquer circumstances in our life. I want you, brothers and sisters, to leave here with a positive attitude. I want you to know that whatever your circumstances are, you can conquer your circumstances.

Circumstance, succumb by things around you, and many of us are surrounded with everything but position your stance. Regardless of what is all around you, God is in the midst of it with you. Do not let your circumstances get you down. We can get the victory. We can conquer our circumstances. If we follow the teachings, if we follow God's teaching, we will be victorious.

The circumstances during Noah's time was the malignant growth of sin. God saw that man's heart was wicked, but God is longsuffering and God is patient with mankind. Noah was living in that day and in that sinful environment where there was a malignant growth of sin. Sin had begun to grow so badly and man's sin had grown so terrible, it seemed there was no check and balance nor no stopping it.

Man was utterly corrupt. Man was bad in his heart, and man was bad in his conduct. Once you have a bad heart, you will say and do bad things. God saw the wickedness of man and God was sorry that he made man. But God saw one man in the midst of those circumstances by the Name of Noah. But Noah found grace in the eyes of the Lord. (Genesis 6:8)

Noah was light in darkness. Where ever there is light darkness vanishes. Noah was that light. He was doing what the Lord said, "Let your light so shine before men that they may see your good works and glorify your Father which is in Heaven." (Matthew 5:16)

I am showing you these truths from Noah's life that can help us conquer our circumstances. You can not afford to succumb to circumstances. Noah was different from anybody else. He was the light in darkness. He was shining. He was doing what the Lord said, "Let your light so shine that men may see your good works and glorify your Father in Heaven." With terrible circumstances all around him, Noah was a conquer. The whole world, at that time, was wicked before God. God was sick that he made man.

We deal with two or three evil or wicked people, and we say but you don't know what I am going through. Look at Noah. Noah lived in a world full of devils. He lived among corruption, wickedness, disobedience, ungodliness, but he found grace in the eyes of the Lord. He did not have to stay there. He could have been like some of us. He could have started acting like the other people around him.

Do not let circumstances squeeze you into a mold of wickedness. Paul said, "And be not conformed to this world: but be ye transformed by the renewing of your mind, that ye may prove what is that good, and acceptable, and perfect, will of God." (Romans 12:2)

Verse 2: *And be not conformed to this world: but be ye transformed by the renewing of your mind, that ye may prove what is that good, and acceptable, and perfect, will of God.*

God's way is not like the world's way. God has a way for the child of God, brothers and sisters, and we cannot do like the world around. We are bought with a price. You are a child of the royal family. The royal children do not play in the alley.

"But ye are a chosen generation, a royal priesthood, an holy nation, a peculiar people; that ye should show forth the praises of him who hath called you out of darkness into his marvelous light:" (I Peter 2:9)

Noah was true to the teachings of the Lord and we should be also. If we are to conquer our circumstances, we must be true to the teachings of the Lord. We have to do what God has said in his word. Nobody forced Noah to be different. Nobody walked behind Noah with a pistol and said, "You had better do right." God did not say to Noah, "You do this or else." God is not going to follow you around and say, "do not go in there; do not pick up this; do not smoke that; do not drink this; do not kiss over here; or feel over there. God's not going to tell you that at all. He is not going to tell you and

God did not tell Noah "obey me or else." Noah had no ultimatums whatsoever.

Noah did have options. It may seem Noah was all along in his commitment but when you think about it, brothers and sisters, Noah was doing what God wanted him to do. Noah was obeying God. It does not make any difference whether you have friends or not; whether people talk about you; they will talk anyway. The most important thing is to know you are in God's plan and you have been doing what God says do. That is joy, my friend.

I enjoy the privilege and I accept the responsibilities that goes with whatever choice I make. I choose to live save. I choose to be baptized in Jesus Name. So, I can accept whatever goes with my choice. That is my choice. I made a decision and I know I am in God will and God's plan for my life. God has got a plan for everybody. You are not here because you thought you would be here. It was God's plan for you to be here. Because you are in the plan of God, it should make you feel good. It makes me happy when I think that I am in the will of God.

Do you not know, brothers and sisters, when you are by yourself, God can get your attention faster, but when people get together, they talk about a lot of things other than God? So, thank God that you are by yourself where

God can talk to you. In some circumstances, God has to put us off by ourselves because when you are in a group of talking people you cannot listen.

God can put you in a position where people will talk about you rather than to you and you will have no one you can talk; just so he can get your attention and put you in a position so you will begin to talk to him. When you find there is no one to talk to, you will cry out, "Lord help me."

I want you to know that God has got a plan for every one of you. You ought to try to make sure you are in the plan of God. When you find out you are in God's will, you may have to cry sometimes, but that is alright. You may have to moan sometimes, but that is alright. It will not last forever. After a while, the Lord will come by and say that enough is enough, my child.

When it looks like there are people who seemingly disregard God's word that God just blesses them. It looks like everything they do is turning for their good. That is what got Asaph in trouble in the 73 Division of Psalms 3,12,16:

Verse 3: *For I was envious at the foolish when I saw the prosperity of the wicked.*

Verse 12: *Behold, these are the ungodly, who prosper in the world; they increase in riches.*

Verse 16: *When I thought to know this, it was too painful for me;*

Verse 17: *Until I went into the sanctuary of God; then understood I their end.*

Some of you are saying," I am doing everything I know how and it look like with all I do, I cannot get ahead. While there are others who are prospering and don't know God." You look at others with new home, new car, new clothes and you say I cannot get ahead. You rationalize that kind of material blessings. Charles Swindoll wrote a book: *Three Steps Forward and Two Back*. You say, it looks like everyone around me is prospering and I take three steps forward and I step back two.

As your pastor, I concluded, many of us have eye trouble. We look and we see nothing but trouble. The Bible says in Colossians 3:2, "Set your affection on things above, not on things on the earth." As your pastor, I say elevate your eyes and look to Jesus. Brothers and sisters, you have got to look beyond trouble, and beyond circumstances. Do not let circumstances frighten you. Do not get upset about your circumstances. Do not count new cars as life. Do not count new homes as living. Do not count a good job as living. Do not count stuff. These are surface things. These are temporal things.

The antediluvian civilization (Luke 17:27) is referenced in Genesis chapter 6:

Verse 5: *And God saw that the wickedness of man was great in the earth and that every imagination of thoughts of his heart was only evil continually.*

Verse 6: *And it repented the Lord that he had made man on the earth and it grieved him at his heart.*

Verse 7: *And the Lord said, I will destroy man whom I have created from the face of the earth; both man, and beast, and the creeping thing, and the fowls of the air; for it repenteth me that I have made them.*

Verse 6: *But Noah found grace in the eyes of the Lord.*

Verse 21: *And take thou unto thee of all food that is eaten, and thou shall gather it to thee; and it shall be for food to thee and for them.*

Verse 22: *Thus did Noah; according to all that God commanded him, so did he.*

When you think about Noah who preached 119 years, or 365 days every year for 119 years, that it is going to rain; come into the ark. Noah was building the ark while he was preaching and nobody listened. Nobody paid Noah any attention. What Noah was preaching made no impression nor indentation on society at all. The Bible says the people kept on partying; they were marrying, giving in marriage, partying and drinking, and having a good time.

Noah kept on building the ark. He kept on telling the people, "It is going to rain". The people kept on partying and ignored Noah's message. The people said, "Old foolish Noah talking about building an ark, it is going to rain. It has never rained."

When you tell anybody you are saved, you are sanctified, you have accepted the Lord Jesus Christ and you have got the Holy Ghost, according to Acts 2:38, they think you have lost your mind. The scripture reads:

Verse 38: *Then Peter said unto them, Repent, and be baptized every one of you in the name of Jesus Christ for the remission of sins, and ye shall receive the gift of the Holy Ghost.*

Verse 39: *For the promise is unto you, and to your children, and to all that are afar off, even as many as the Lord our God shall call.*

Verse 40: *And with many other words did he testify and exhort, saying Save yourselves from this untoward generation.*

Verse 41: *Then they that gladly received this word were baptized and the same day there were added unto them about three thousand souls.*

You can go anywhere, join anything, but when you say I have been baptized in Jesus Name, I am Holy Ghost filled, people will say, you must have lost your mind.

We are impressed with what people think. Noah kept on building the ark. When you are trying to do something for God and it seems nobody is going along with you, it makes you wonder whether you are doing a right thing or not. Do not worry about what people say; if you know you are doing God's will and you know you did not do any manipulating, scheming, giving or trying to make or create an ideal situation for yourself, then you know God put you where you are for a reason. You stay there until God is through using you and God will take you out of the situation.

God can tell the devil, take your hands off and don't bother you. The Bible says in II Timothy 2:19:

Verse 19: *Nevertheless the foundation of God standeth sure, having this seal, The Lord knoweth them that are his. And, Let everyone that nameth the name of Christ depart from iniquity. God know you, my friend.*

Paul says in II Timothy 1:12-14:

Verse 12: *For the which cause I also suffer these things: nevertheless, I am not ashamed: for I know whom I have believed, and am persuaded that he is able to keep that which I have committed unto him against that day.*

Verse 13: *Hold fast the form of sound words, which thou hast heard of me, in faith and love which is in Christ Jesus.*

Verse 14: *That good thing which was committed unto thee keep by the Holy Ghost which dwelleth in us.*

I am talking about conquering circumstances.

Nobody cared what Noah did, but Noah did what God told him to do, he built the ark. Noah obeyed God.

Matthew 16:26-27:

Verse 26: *For what is a man profited, if he shall gain the whole world, and lose his own soul? Or what shall a man give in exchange for his soul?*

Verse 27: *For the Son of man shall come in his glory of his Father with his angels; and then he shall reward every man according to his works.*

Brothers and Sisters, you had better obey the teachings of God. If you want to conquer circumstances, follow the teachings of God.

In Genesis 6:22, Noah did according to all that God commanded him, so did he.

God had instructed Noah what to do. He followed the leadership of God. But the problem with us when we get in some circumstances, you panic, run, cry, fall out and kick, go into hysteria like a child. You cannot do that, many of us do, but you can stand up and take a real view of your circumstances and say, "Now Lord, what would you have me to do?"

Thus, did Noah according to all that God commanded him, so did he. (Genesis 6:22)

Noah conquered by following leadership and being obedient. The songwriter wrote: "When we walk with the Lord in the light of his word, what a glory he sheds on our way. While we do his good will, he abides with us still, and with all who will trust and obey. Trust and obey for there's no other way to be happy in Jesus but to trust and obey." Obedience is key.

Jesus said in St Luke 6:46: Verse 46: And why call ye me, Lord, Lord, and do not the things which I say?

If we are not following the leadership of God, not doing the things God says do, not obeying God, why call him Lord, Lord, Lord and not do what he says. Herein lies the victory in your circumstances when we do what God says do. I am talking about how you can get the victory. You can get victory in your circumstances by following the leadership of God. We must stop looking at our circumstances and start looking to God.

I am reminded of the story of Elisha when he was in Dothan, II Kings 6:15-17:

Verse 15: *And when the servant of the man of God was risen early, and gone forth behold, an host compassed the city both with horses and chariots. And his servant said unto him, Alas, my master! How shall we do?*

Verse 16: *And he answered, Fear not: for they that be with us are more than they that be with them.*

Verse 17: *And Elisha prayed, and said, Lord, I pray thee, open his eyes, that he may see. And the Lord opened the eyes of the young man; and he saw; and, behold, the mountain was full of horses and chariots of fire round about Elisha.*

You have to understand, brothers and sisters, God has given us the capacity to look beyond wickedness in this corrupt world in which we live. You see you can look beyond all this turmoil here and see God. Now you may not see God in it, but I can see God in it. When you look around at all the wickedness, God has given you the capacity to look beyond wickedness, evilness, corruption and sinfulness in this world, you do not have to be caught up with that kind of stuff, it doesn't have to brother you.

You see, many times we are all upset because we do not know God is still working. God is working. There is never a time when God is not working. God does not take any breaks. God does not go on vacations. God doesn't have any days off. God doesn't work the third shift this week and the first shift the next week. God is always working. God is never off. God is always workings. There is never a time when God is not working in this world. In the darkest moments, God is working. We can be sure that God is at work. Anytime you think about it, God is at work.

The Bible made it quite plain in II Kings, 6: 6, 15, 16, 17:

Verse 6: *And the man of God said, "Where fell it?" And he shewed him the place. And he cut down a stick, and cast it in thither; and the iron did swim.*

Verse 15: *And when the servant of the man of God was risen early, and gone forth, behold, an host compassed the city both with horses and chariots. And his servant said unto him, Alas, my master! How shall we do?*

Verse 16: *And he answered, Fear not: for they that be with us are more than they that be with them.*

Verse 17: *And Elisha prayed, and said, Lord, I pray thee, open his eyes that he may see. And Lord the opened the eyes of the young man; and he saw: and, behold, the mountain was full of horses and chariots of fire round about Elisha.*

Now here was the man of God, Elisha and his servant that got excited; "And when the servant of the man of God was risen early and gone forth, behold a host compassed the city both with horses and chariots."

Now picture these circumstances, you wake up in the morning and Chicago is surrounded by Russians. You are all hemmed in. Fidel Castro is 80 miles off the East coast. When Fidel Castro came into power this country got all upset. Some things, after a long period of time, you learn how to live with it. You do not get any victory over it, but you learn how to live with it because you cannot do nothing about it any way.

But with this man of God, God is working and that is what you need to understand. God is working when you do not think he is working. God is working behind the scenes. God is out of sight many times. God is working on people's heart and you do not know God is working. This man got up that morning and looked out there and saw the city compassed about with horses and chariots. "And his servant said unto him, Alas, my master! How shall we do?"

Now, have you been in some circumstances and you did not ask God, you asked somebody else, what can I do? But here this man of God, got up that morning, looked out there and saw the mountainside all around the city, horses and chariots. They were all locked in; they went back to the man of God and said, "Master, what are we going to do?" What are we going to do? This is a circumstance that we are in and I do not know how to get out of it. I do not know what to do with this one. There are only two of us here, just you and I; now, what are we going to do?

When you know you have the victory, brothers and sisters, when you know you are in tune with God, when you know you have been living right, when you know that God is working, and when you know that God did not have to work, God has already worked. Elisha answered, "Fear not, in other words, calm down, do not get excited. Do not be afraid. "For they that be with us are more than they that be with them."

Now, he looked out there and saw the horses all around the city. He looked out there and saw all the chariots. He did not see nobody working, but I want you to know God was working. You may not see it, brothers and sisters, but God is working behind the scenes. Elisha says, look here, we got more with us than be with them.

"Elisha prayed, and said, Lord, I ask you, open his eyes that he may see." Many people need their eyes opened. They do not see God working. They are complaining all the time. They do not see God anywhere.

Well, do not worry, God is working. Do not get upset. Nobody can do you harm unless God let them touch you. The devil can not do nothing but look at you. If God says do not touch you, then the devil can not touch you. Do not get upset. Elisha said, "Open his eyes that he might see." You need to see God working. You need to see God's hand working. You need to see bodyguards. You need to see your security. You need to see God's protection.

"And the Lord opened the eyes of the young man and he saw and behold, the mountain was full of horses and chariots of fire." They had only horses and chariots, but we have horses, chariots and fire around about Elisha. You see when you stand all by yourself, you are never alone. The songwriter wrote the song, "Never Alone, No Never Alone; He promised never to leave me, never to leave me alone." You may not be able to see it, but you are never alone. You may not be able to see it, but you are never alone.

And the Lord said, "Open his eyes and let him see." And he looked around and saw all the horses all around the mountains. He saw all the chariots and the fire. We are singing the song "Nobody knows the trouble I see." God is on your side. Do not worry. Paul said, if God be for us, that is more than the whole world against you.

Romans 8:31, 37:

Verse 31: *What shall we then say to these things? If God be for us, who can be against us?*

Verse 37: *Nay, in all these things we are more than conquerors through him that loved us.*

Do not worry about circumstances. Let us conquer our circumstances. Let us follow the teachings of God. Let us follow the leadership of God. Let us obey God's word. Let us trust God and God will give you the victory. I am saying, my friend, whatever your circumstances are, you can get the victory by following the word of God.

I do not know your circumstances, but you can conquer your circumstances. You can conquer it. Defy the devil. Pray this prayer, "Loose here Satan, in the Name of Jesus."

Conquering Circumstances: Circumstances are things that you find yourself surround with. You are surrounded, you are standing and the devil is all around you. People looking at you and you are wondering what am I going to do. It is time.

There is somebody here who has a need. You have a problem. In some circumstances you do not know what will happen, but I am saying, you can have the victory in your circumstances. Find God's word and stand on God's word. That is all Noah had was God's word. He did not have anything but God's word. God told Noah to build an ark, it is going to rain. And the Bible said, "Noah found grace in the eyes of the Lord."

Many of you have circumstances on your job, in your home. The devil is raging everywhere. Do you not know these are the last days? The scripture did not promise, in time, things would get better. It did say, perilous times would come. The world is more wick and wiser. With technology, doctors can put livers, kidneys and hearts in people. Soon, we will be manufacturing body parts and organs to make a man. When God says live, you will live. The Bible says God has appointed a day and every man, every woman, is going to stand before the judgment seat of Christ to give an account of the deeds done in their body.

Conquering Temptations

Welcome to "Super Conquerors" the second lesson of a six-part series. For clarity, in the book of Genesis Chapter 39: 1–9, I want you to reflect on God's goodness to you as we read these verses together.

GENESIS CHAPTER 39: 1–9

Joseph Tested by Adversity

Verse 1: *And Joseph was brought down to Egypt; and Potiphar, an officer of Pharaoh, captain of the guard, an Egyptian, bought him of the hands of the Ishmaelites, which had brought him down thither.*

Verse 2: *And the Lord was with Joseph, and he was a prosperous man; and he was in the house of his master the Egyptian.*

Verse 3: *And his master saw that the Lord was with him, and that the Lord made all that he did to prosper in his hand.*

Verse 4: *And Joseph found grace in his sight, and he served him: and he made him overseer over his house, and all that he had he put into his hand.*

Verse 5: *And it came to pass from the time that he had made him overseer in his house, and over all that he had, that the lord blessed the Egyptian's house for Joseph's sake; and the blessing of the Lord was upon all that he had in the house and in the field.*

Verse 6: *And he left all that he had in Joseph's hand; and he knew not ought he had, save the bread which he did eat. And Joseph was a goodly person, and well favoured.*

Verse 7: *And it came to pass after these things, that his master's wife cast her eyes upon Joseph; and she said, Lie with me.*

Verse 8: *But he refused, and said unto his master's wife, Behold, my master wotteth not what is with me in the house, and he hath committed all that he hath to my hand;*

Verse 9: *There is none greater in this house than I; neither hath he kept back anything from me but thee because thou art his wife: how then can I do this great wickedness and sin against God?*

I want you to remember that we are still conquering. How many super conquerors do we have here? Are you a super conqueror? How many have already lost your super conquering title? Do you think the Satan has taken your title from you? All super conquerors stand to your feet. Tell the devil you have got him down. Now you keep him on the floor and put your foot on him. You have the victory!

If you are going to be a super conqueror that means you have to be a conqueror in every area of your life. Now, we are trying to find out whether you are still maintaining your super conqueror title.

Last week we talked about "Conquering Circumstances." How many found you had some circumstances you had to conquer? Did you do alright with conquering your circumstances? Did you come through with the victory? Then, "Thank the Lord."

This week we are conquering temptations

Tell somebody, "We are conquering temptations." Thank you, Jesus. I know that all of us are claiming to be super conquerors; everybody is claiming to be a super conqueror. That is alright with me. I want you to be a super conqueror.

I am and I will be speaking about conquering some areas that we may think we have already conquered. I am positive there are some circumstances you thought you had conquered and later you found out, you had not conquered those circumstances at all.

Well today, you maybe conquering those circumstances. There are some temptations that you are going to have to conquer and we cannot claim the status of a super conqueror until we are conquerors in all areas of your life.

There are world champions in many fields of sports. We have basketball champions; We have football champions. We have soccer champions. We have champions who defeat all the other teams that were excellent teams. Champions are the best of the best. The champions raise above all the other teams. They actually defeated all the other teams.

So, if you are a super conqueror, that means you should defeat many things and you should be a champion. You should be a conqueror that have overcome many things. Is that so?

Well alright, we are going to claim being a conqueror anyway. If there are some areas in life you have not conquered yet, you are not worthy to be called a super conqueror. You are one of the generic conquerors. You are not the real thing.

You are out there playing like a lot of bad dogs who claim to be bad dogs. They bark as long as they are chained. You turn them loose and stomp your foot at them and they run. I do not want you to be that kind of conqueror.

So today, with God's help, brothers and sisters, let us look at temptations which can help you or destroy you. It depends on what you do with the temptations. Now temptations can help you or temptations can destroy you. It is left entirely to you what temptations does. No one can decide that but you. You have to make that decision.

And in these verses, we have before us, we find in the life of Joseph, what I believe, will help you with temptations. I believe it will. Are you aware that one of the greatest surprises to new children of God is that they still have temptations? That is one of the greatest surprises that come to new saints and a whole lot of older saints too, that they still have temptations, and that you still can be tempted and that you are tempted.

I wonder, are you aware of that? Most times we feel it will never, never happen to me. I will never have that problem again. I am saved; I am a Christian and the things I use to do I don't do now, so I won't have any more problems.

I use to drink, but I do not have to worry about drinking any more. I am saved now. That is true, but I have news for you. Many times, you are watching television and you see people drinking beer and cold cocktails; somehow your mind goes back to when you use to indulge. It seems you can almost taste one of those beers or margaritas. Amen. There will be nobody to say nothing except for those people who know what margaritas are. Amen. Amen. Thank the Lord. *That is what happens.* Temptation is real, brothers and sisters.

I use to smoke a pack of cigarettes or more a day. After I had been saved for several years, I woke up one morning and it seem like I had smoked cigarettes all night in my dream while asleep. It was so real to me. I woke up looking for the cigarettes. I really did. I was looking for the cigarettes. I felt so condemned when I awaken. I said, "Now, you are saved. You are not supposed to smoke." And I said, "That's right, I am not; but I was looking for the cigarettes."

The devil was manipulating my mind. The temptation was so strong that I thought I had really smoked. I have never heard of anybody smoking in their sleep. But it just goes to show you how real a dream can be and the ways temptation can present itself.

You will find that temptations are still real, brothers and sisters, those problems you thought were gone are still there. Now, what are you going to do with them? That's the question. Because you have accepted Jesus Christ as your Lord and Savior, does not change the problem. The only thing Jesus has done is given you somebody to help you with the problem. Learn how to cast your cares on Jesus and let Jesus deal with the problem.

To think you will have no problems; no temptations, nothing could be further from the truth. You will have problems. There will always be temptations for the child of God and especially those that are living right.

Those who are yielding to temptations and living any kind of way, you are not going to have any problems with the devil. Yes, you are going to have some problems, then, because the devil doesn't really want to just get you down; he really wants to kill you. And that is what his job is to steal, kill and destroy.

(John 10:10)

Verse 10: *The thief cometh not, but for to steal, and to kill, and to destroy: I am come that they might have life, and that they might have it more abundantly.*

But in all of the temptations you have, various types and scopes, your temptations will be changing to some degree, but they will never fully depart. Temptations will always be there.

When you look at the house of Potiphar, there is Joseph, a young boy, real handsome and in his youth. His father loved Joseph more than the rest of his sons. (Genesis 37:3) The father spoiled Joseph, in a sense. Joseph did not have to work. The other sons were out in the field working.

Before Joseph got to Potiphar's house, Joseph had a lot of misfortune. His Father, Israel, made his brothers hate him. (Genesis 37:11)

Even being sold by his brothers, God brought Joseph out of the pit where his brothers had placed him. (Genesis 37:20)

Joseph, who was brought to Potiphar's house, because he was sold by his brothers. (Genesis 37:27)

God carried Joseph down in Egypt and Joseph ended up in Potiphar's house. Joseph was living among luxury, fine living and good times. After all, Potiphar was the captain of the guards. (Genesis 37:36)

Therefore, we know Joseph lived in the royal palace, on the royal ground, and in the royal domain. He had some good things. Joseph worked in his house and Joseph was there but he was tempted. Joseph faced his temptation and conquered his temptation.

Every temptation thrown at Joseph, he conquered it. He didn't succumb to any of them. From Joseph's experiences, we can find four truths in this particular lesson that I think would be very necessary, and very good for you and it will help you with your temptations. I don't want you to miss these truths either. I want you to catch every one of them.

Number one: Understand and recognize <u>temptations are not sinful.</u>

Number two: Understand and recognize the <u>goal of temptations.</u>

Number three: Understand and recognize the <u>aims of temptations.</u>

Number four: Understand and recognize the
                <u>power of temptations</u>.

These are the four things that you need to understand. And after you realize that temptations are not sinful, realize the aim; realize the goal and realize that temptations do have power. You need to understand temptations and claim the victory in the temptation. You can go forward and continue to walk with God.

This is what we are going to have to do, brothers and sisters, if we are going to be victorious. I do not want you to go through life thinking you are not going to have any problems. You are going to have some problems. All of our problems are not at the address where you reside nor are all of your problems on the job where you work. You may be sitting among people who are experiencing temptations.

Temptations are not sinful, but you know what, Satan will try to make you feel that they are. You will find some temptations come your way, however, Satan does a very good job to make you feel that your temptations are sinful.

Some desires you have are natural desires that God meant for you to have, but when you pervert the natural desire that makes it bad.

Pervert means to change something so that it is not what it was or should be; pervert is a person with abnormal sexual behavior. An example of a pervert is someone who peeks into his or her neighbor's bathroom. It is not so much the desire as it is what you do with the desire. Now you can overextend this desire and pervert it.

The purpose that God meant for you to use temptation is for your benefit, you can use it otherwise and you can get in trouble.

Temptations. Satan tries to make you believe that they are sinful and that they are bad and if he can convince you of that, he can sell you the idea that the temptation that you had, is sinful, and is bad, Satan got you. You will then beunder the power of Satan. He will have you on the way to defeat. Once he gets you like that, thinking that the temptations are sinful, Satan has a good start on the way to defeating you in whatever he is going to do, and you are going to lose out too. He can defeat you in your spiritual life with God. Our spiritual life is the thing that is important. You have got to understand that you must start getting some victory over temptations.

You have heard it said, "You cannot stop birds from flying over your head, but do not let them make a nest in your head."

Ideas are going to come, but you have to be able to push the ideas out of your mind. You don't have to entertain the ideas to make them become real. You have to understand that the devil is trying to influence you, trying to get you under his power and give you a defeated attitude where you feel that you are in sin. Well you are not in sin until you sin.

Nobody can sin by thinking about sin, but when sin can capture you and you begin to carry out what sin does.

Our lesson two is talking about, temptations. Joseph did not sin because he was tempted by Potiphar's wife. He did not sin because she tempted him. She tempted him!

Joseph had been in Potiphar's house for 10 years. She watched Joseph grow. The Bible says, "Everything Joseph did God prospered him." She saw Joseph being blessed there. This woman saw Joseph. This handsome young man. This beautiful young man. The Bible said, "He was handsome." Joseph was handsome and young. A young man who had great favor in the house of Potiphar. This woman looked upon Joseph and she just did not ask him one time, brothers and sisters, she did not ask him just one time to lay with her. The Bible says she asked him day by day. Constantly saying, "Joseph."

She was alluring and very attractive; tempting; enticing; seductive; exciting, beguiling, captivating, and bewitching.

Can you imagine the captain of the guard's wife dressed in a very sheer negligee trying to seduce Joseph? But this young Hebrew boy, in Potiphar's house, realized that God had put him there. Later, we know God had him there for a purpose. You need to understand, brothers and sisters, because of who you are, does not exempt you from temptation; does not exempt you from trouble.

You can walk around saying you are sanctified and set aside for the Masters' use, and you can speak in tongues, but that does not change the devil's mind about you at all. The devil is not moved because you are sanctified. You have to show him you have some power with God. Speaking in tongues does not mean a lot to the devil. The devil can speak in tongues, but you have to know, when you stop speaking in tongues, brothers and sisters, you must be able to have some power to say "No!" to what the devil presents. When the devil brings temptation, you must be able to say, "No, I don't want it; get away from me!" Don't even look at it.

I find nowhere in the Bible where Joseph began to entertain and enjoy what was being said. After all, here is

Joseph, a young boy, who has everything going for him and here is his bosses' wife saying, "Come, Joseph, lay with me."

Now, if you heard this day by day, someone saying, "Come lay with me." "Come on Joseph, I want you to lay with me". "I want you to lie down with me, Joseph." And Joseph kept on walking by and ignoring the temptation.

I can understand, one time, but this was a constant thing. The devil knows how to keep bombarding you with temptation all the time. When the devil knows you are a sex fiend, defined as an evil spirit or a demon; that is what the devil will let you see, people naked all the time. That is what the devil will do.

If you like to drink, the devil will let you see people drinking all the time. The devil will make it convenient for you to something to drink. You have to be able to say," no! no! no!" And I mean, no!

You cannot play with the devil, brothers and sisters. A lot of young women have got in trouble because they did not know how to say, no! You cannot play with the devil. When someone is trying to seduce you, you tell them, take your hands off me! Leave me alone! Get out of my face! I am not going to be tempted like that. I am not going to see myself out for a little cheap fun like that! But the devil keeps on coming to you. You have to be able to say No! No! No! All the time Joseph said, "No," but Potiphar's wife did not believe Joseph meant no.

Finally, the Bible says, one day…you see many times, we need to understand that sin leads to temptations. Although it might lead to temptation, generally when you pervert the temptation, you see it is nothing to desire a woman or to desire a man. God gives you the parameters for the desire. God just does not say, everyone you see and want, you can have. It is not like that. God told you every man has his own wife and every woman her own husband.

I Corinthians 7:3

Verse 3: *Let the husband render unto the wife due benevolence; and likewise, also the wife unto the husband.*

You don't dip and dab over here in the church, brothers and sisters, and go to heaven.

I want you to know that temptation was not a sign of weakness. Joseph in his position had influence. The temptation was not there because he had an encounter with temptation. All temptation is not wicked but the devil will try to seduce you. Joseph, in his position, had great influence. That is all the devil would like to do with you, as a child of God, is to mar or kill your influence.

All we have is influence. We say, "I am a child of God; God picked me up out of the muck and mire; washed me in his blood; gave me the Holy Ghost and sent me on my way rejoicing." Now you are walking around saying I am sanctified, got the Holy Ghost, baptized in Jesus Name and I don't do this or I don't do the other. Well the devil says," I am going to find out whether you will do this or if you will do the other."

So, people are watching you. When you get saved and when you take a stand for Jesus, people are watching you. They want to see whether you are for real or not.

The devil can kill your influence. That is all he wants to do. He will not altogether kill you, but he wants to kill your influence. The devil does not want anyone to listen to you or pay attention to what you say you believe. The devil wants people to think you are all talk and no substance.

In conclusion, you *can* conquer temptations.

SUPER CONQUERORS

Conquering Fear

Welcome to "Super Conquerors"
the third lesson of a six-part series.

2 Timothy, Chapter 1: 1-7
Part I. The Apostolic Greeting.

Our lesson is on conquering fear. Read what Paul said to his son, Timothy in 2 Timothy, Chapter 1:1-7:

Verse 1: *Paul, an apostle of Jesus Chris Christ by the will of God, according to the promise of life which is in Christ Jesus,*

Verse 2: To *Timothy, my dearly beloved son: Grace, mercy, and peace, from God the Father and Christ Jesus our Lord.*

Verse 3: *I thank God, whom I serve from my forefathers with pure conscience, that without ceasing I have remembrance of thee in my prayers night and day;*

Verse 4: *Greatly desiring to see thee, being mindful of thy tears, that I may be filled with joy;*

Verse 5: *When I call to remembrance the unfeigned faith that is in three, which dwelt first in thy grandmother Lois, and thy mother Eunice; and I am persuaded that in thee also.*

Verse 6: *Wherefore I put thee in remembrance that thou stir up the gift of God, which is in thee by the putting on of my hands.*

Verse 7: *For God hath not given us the spirit of fear; but of power, and of love and of a sound mind.*

Conquering fear. If the disciples had stirred up the gift of God which is in them, they would not have had trouble on that Easter Sunday, but they had not conquered fear.

When I think about what happened to the disciples of Jesus after he was crucified, the disciples got very sad; the disciples went into hiding behind closed doors because of fear and did not come out. Nobody believed us. It is impossible. He is gone so that is all it is to it. I am not going to worry about it at all. Not going to worry about it. They went their way. They were afraid for their lives. They didn't want anyone to know they had been associated with Jesus. Fear is dangerous, brothers and sisters.

Easter Sunday came and found Jesus disciples sad and afraid. They were very sad and afraid. They killed our Master. They got rid of our bread ticket. They got rid of our joy giver. He is no longer around. I am wondering how many of you here have conquered fear? Are you plagued by fear from day to day? It is nothing to be ashamed of if you have not conquered fear. You have to learn how to conquer it. Have you ever been afraid? Just a few questions I will ask you. I know all of your answers will be in the affirmative.

1. Have you ever been afraid?

2. Do you know the unpleasant truth that fear is the robber of all spiritual joy?

3. Fear is the robber of all spiritual joys, did you know that?

4. Have fear caused you to do some very strange things?

5. Fear causes people to do some very strange things. It is terrible, isn't it?

6. Do you want to able to conquer fear?

Would you like to be able to conquer fear?

You should want to be able to conquer fear. These questions, I am sure, will receive a very responsive "yes" to every one of them. But in the spirit of, the excellent family heritage that Timothy had, this religious training was beautiful. The wonderful friends he had was excellent. The personal experiences he had were great thing to have.

Timothy had many responsibilities and sincerities, but Timothy was really very timid and fearful. If you read the scriptures very closely, he was timid by nature. He desperately needed help in conquering fear. Someone who is already timid needs somebody to give him some backbone. For if he did not get come help to learn how to conquer fear, he would become defeated in trying to serve God. He would not be able to do what he wanted to do.

Since Paul's words were part counseling and part encouragement, is words came at just the right time for Timothy. Sometimes we get the help at the right time. Sometimes it looks like we are just waiting for somebody to come along and say just the right words to us and that will help us.

Paul came along at just the right time to help Timothy. We can know that there is help. There is help to conquer fear. If there was no help to conquer fear, brothers and sisters, we would be in a most miserable, condition because most of us fear for what tomorrow holds. Now some have not gone quite that far. Some are afraid to go back home because of the situation you left there. The situation you left at home was not conducive for you to go back and expect it to be resolved by you going away.

Any of you have things you are thinking about that keep you in a miserable state and from enjoying the blessings of God. When we think about it, there are two basic facts which we need to conquer our fears. There are two things that we must use to conquer fear. If we are going to conquer fear, we have got to use these things.

First thing, you need to know is that Satan is the author of fear. That is the first thing.

Now you need to know that there are two kinds of fear that are prevalent among the people of God. Satan is the author of fear. Certainly, we ought to know that.

One of these we ought to have and it should be at work in our lives.

1. We should be afraid to break the laws of God. That is number one.

2. You should be afraid to break the laws of nature.

3. You should be afraid to break the laws of the
   state.

Breaking God's law is dangerous. Breaking the laws of nature, you are going to pay for it. Now if you don't believe that, one of the laws of nature is the law of gravity. Open the window and jump out and see won't you go down. I want you to understand what I am saying, brothers and sisters. Fear can be helpful and good, but we should not want to break God's law. I should be fearful of breaking God's law; even nature laws.

I don't want to break the laws of the State of Illinois because there is Joliet and there is 26th Street and there is Wentworth Avenue all of these are holding areas until they can send you some place to do your time for breaking the laws of the state. Everybody ought to be fearful of that.

Not only should we be fearful of breaking God's law, but the other thing we ought to fear is the destructiveness. Fear is damaging to the body. Fear is damaging to the mind.

Fear is damaging to the soul of man. It has troubled man ever since Adam. Man has been troubled by fear ever since the days of Adam. It causes many people to live in a haunted bondage and they are afraid to come out. People are constantly dreading what the outcome maybe.

People are always worried. Some of the things they are dreading are real but most of them are imagination that getsthe best of them. People worry about the outcome of things that you have no control over at all, brothers and sisters.

Many a time if you would just be patient, just be calm, and just trust God, things will work itself out. But people worry about it, and this is caused by Satan. Satan causes you to worry about things that you can't control. Satan makes you fear the worst of everything. He lets you see the worst of all things. If you could see the good in a lot of things, you would change. Because you don't see nothing, but bad things; then Satan is the author or paints pictures of bad things. So, you don't see the good that comes out of some of these bad things. Consequently, you miss out and you are miserable.

You are constantly worrying about what is going to happen. You are afraid. You are afraid. Not only must you know Satan is author of fear, but you need to know his purpose for fear. You need to know his purpose for this kind of fear that he brings on the child of God.

As its author, Satan has a real purpose in doing what he does. He has a purpose. He wants to put fear in your mind so that we remain afraid. Satan does not want you to serve God.

Now if you can get some confidence in your mind, there are a lot of people who will get up and accept Jesus as the Saviour. Perhaps people are fearful of what people were going to say when they go home. A whole lot of people would get baptized in Jesus Name if they were not fearful of something.

For example, "I don't know what my mom is going to say. After all, we have been in this Baptist Church, or this Methodist Church for a long time." One young woman told me, "All my family goes church." So, what if all her family goes to church. All my family went to Mount Ebenezer Baptist Church. They all went there. I left there.

A lot of people's relatives go to prison. Are you going to prison? All my brothers, all my cousins are in prison, I am going too. No, it doesn't work like that. That is fear.

What we need to understand is that Satan has a purpose and his greatest purpose to instill fear in the heart of God's people. Then his purpose can be better understood, brothers and sisters. When people realize this fear comes to make us fearful or timid. He uses the spirit of fearfulness and timidity to stop you.

Not a lot of people are naturally timid. People who are naturally timid and fearful have problems, too. They are not going to do anything.

One of the things, as a minister, you have to get over is the fear of asking for money because people, people will say, "Oh, they talk about money all the time." I understand that money is needed to operate this church, so I have got to ask for it. So, your looking does not bother me now. It used to bother me, but it does not bother me now. My fear vanished. I had to conquer that fear.

SUPER CONQUERORS

Conquering Discouragement

Welcome to "Super Conquerors"
the fourth lesson of a six-part series.

I King, Chapter 19: 1-15
Jehovah's tender care of His overwrought prophet.

Our lesson is on conquering Discouragement. Read I King, Chapter 19:1-15:

Verse 1: *And Ahab told Jezebel all that Elijah had done, and withal how he had slain all the prophets with the sword.*

Verse 2: *Then Jezebel sent a messenger unto Elijah, saying, So let the gods do to me, and more also, if I make not thy life as the life of one of them by to morrow about this time.*

Verse 3: *And when he saw that, he arose, and went for his life and came to Beer-sheba, which belongeth to Juda, and left his servant there.*

Verse 4: *But he himself went a day's journey into the wilderness, and came and sat down under a juniper tree: and he requested for himself that he might die; and said, It's enough; now, O Lord, take away my life; for I am not better than my fathers.*

Verse 5: *And as he lay and slept under a juniper tree, behold, then an angel touched him, and said unto him, Arise and eat.*

Verse 6: *And he looked, and, behold, there was a cake baken on the coals, and a cruse of water at his head. And he did eat and drink, and laid him down again.*

Verse 7: *And the angel of the Lord came again the second time, and touched him, and said, Arise and eat; because the journey is too great for thee.*

Elijah on Horeb.

Verse 8: *And he arose, and did eat and drink, and went in the strength of that meat forty days and forty nights unto Horeb the mount of God.*

Verse 9: *And he came thither unto a cave, and lodged there; and, behold, the word of the Lord came to him, and he said unto him, What doest thou here, Elijah?*

Verse 10: *And he said, I have been very jealous for the Lord God of hosts: for the children of Israel have forsaken thy covenant, thrown down thine altars, and slain thy prophets with the sword and I, even I only, am left; and they seek my life, to take it away.*

Verse 11: *And he said, "Go forth, and stand upon the mount before the Lord." And, behold, the Lord passed by, and a great and strong wind rent the mountains, and brake in pieces the rocks before the Lord; but the Lord was not in the wind: and after the wind an earthquake; but the Lord was not in the earthquake:*

Verse 12: *And after the earthquake a fire; but the Lord was not in the: and after the fire a still small voice.*

Verse 13: *And it was so, when Elijah heard it, that he wrapped his face in his mantle, and went out, and stood in the entering in of the cave.*

Verse 14: *And he said, I have been very jealous for the Lord God of hosts: because the children of Israel have forsaken thy covenant, thrown down thine altars, and slain thy prophets with the sword; and I even I only, am left; and they seek my life, to take it away.*

Verse 15: *And the Lord said unto him, Go, return on thy way to the wilderness of Damascus: and when thou comest, anoint Hazael to be king over Syria:*

Let us focus on verse 14, "And he said, I have been very jealous for the Lord God of hosts: because the children of Israel have forsaken thy covenant, thrown down thine altars, and slain thy prophets with the sword; and I, even I only, am left; and they seek my life, to take it away.

This lesson is about "Conquering Discouragement." There were several lessons and each one had a title. All of you were given these titles. You were told that you are a super conqueror. If you intend to maintain your title, you must conquer the attributes of a conqueror. Lesson one: Conquer Circumstances; Lesson two: Conquer Temptation; and Lesson three: Conquer Fear. This lesson is on conquering discouragement. You have to maintain the attributes of a conqueror or you must give up your title of becoming a super conqueror.

Everyone has experienced discouragement. If I asked, by a show of hands, how many are experiencing discouragement? Many of you are experiencing discouragement and you must confess that discouragement is chaotic. Discouragement is hopeless. It is terrible. It is desperate. It is despondency. It is depression and a form of dejection. All of these words are nouns and synonyms for discouragement. These words express an emotional state when there is a low spirit or a loss of hope.

Some of you have been in the position of feeling there is no hope for you. Discouragement comes in many forms. Some may say, "It looks like I am never going to get a job." Some may say, "I am always going to have some aches and pains." Others may say, I am always short on money."

Some people like to cry or complain; they may think it is a way to get people to feel sorry for them. Some people have childish ways or traits. They want attention and this is one way to get people feeling sorry for them. They feel sorry for themselves. They always have a sad story to tell. They cannot see the sunshine; it is always a cloudy day or stormy weather.

Will you think with me, especially those of you who might need to be encouraged and those of you who want to conquer discouragement.

Are some of these sayings and experiences familiar to you? "I quit." "I am fed up." "I can't take any more." "No one seems to care about me at all." In our lesson, that sounds like Elijah. Elijah said, "I had enough. I am fed up. I cannot take any more. You do not care about."

Can you imagine Elijah telling that to the very God of heaven? Elijah had just killed all of Baal's prophets and devoured them upon Mt Carmel. Ahab went back and said, "Look what this man, Elijah, has done to us." Jezebel said, "Give me some paper. Go back and tell him, I am going to do the same thing to him about this time tomorrow." When Elijah heard this, the Bible says he took off towards the South, running for his life.

Where was Elijah's nerves? A threat had caused Elijah to lose all his hope. Elijah lost all hope and became upset. Despondency and discouragement are caused by a low spirit or loss of hope. These are causes for this emotional state. There is no need for a child of God to allow himself to be lowered into a state that you cannot trust God or a state that would cause you to say, "I quit." "I am fed up." "Nobody cares about me."

Anger can cause you to speak sayings like that. These are words and statements that discouraged people will speak. These are utterances of most discouraged people in a saddened state. When one gets to that state, most of the times you are really angry with someone.

Not all discouraged people speak of their discouragement. Some people just reveal it silently in their lifestyle. Sometimes you can tell they are going through something by their body language or by their silence.

They are not making a whole lot of fuss; not talking about their situation; but just going through silently.

Discouragement is easily found in schools, in governments, in offices, in homes, in factories and even in churches. It is safe to say, brothers and sisters, anywhere you find people, you find discouragement. Somebody is going to lose hope. Someone does not feel like going forward. You will also find discouragement causes many people to go to their grave.

Discouragement will claim at least 95% of today's people and discouragement will be the cause of many people going by the way of the grave.

From the beginning of time, discouragement has been one of Satan's primary weapons, and one of the most effective weapons that he uses again the people of God.

Satan always brings something to you that causes you to be discouraged. People who are discouraged are constantly saying things to keep themselves

discouraged. For instance, "I am fed up, I quit, I cannot take it anymore. Nobody cares about me."

Discouragement is one form of hopelessness. No hope at all. People who are hopeless have no hope at all. People who are hopeless have no hope, no joy and are most often subject to discouragement. If you do not want to be discouraged, you need to find someone who does not speak in a discouraging manner. You have to learn when to leave people who discourage you alone

When you read I Kings 19 it says, "You can conquer discouragement." If it says anything to modern man, to you and me, it tells us you can conquer discouragement.

You may not believe it. You may not see it. To me, it says you can conquer discouragement. You can conquer your discouragements, too. You can move to victory in God and enjoy the victories of God if you conquer discouragement.

The question that comes to mind is this, "Do you want to know how to conquer discouragement? Some people may not want to know how to conquer discouragement. You may be satisfied with where you are with seeking attention, but if you are to gain the victory over discouragement, you will have to face lifefor themselves. If you want to know how to gain victory over discouragement, then the life of Elijah reveals three things that we must do in order to become a conqueror of discouragement.

When you look at Elijah's life, it reveals three thing that we as saints of God can do to become a conqueror over discouragement.

1. Recognize Causes

2. Recognize Physical Causes

3. Recognize Spiritual Causes

Recognize Causes: There is a cause for discouragement. There is a reason for discouragement. God, in his inspired word, has revealed to us the causes for Elijah's discouragement. The things that caused Elijah to be discouraged are the same things people face today.

As recorded in the book of James 5:17:

Verse 17: *Elias was a man subject to like passions as we are, and he prayed earnestly that it might not rain; and it rained not on the earth by the space of three years and six months.*

Elias, Greek form of Elijah in the New Testament, James 5:17 and Elijah in the old testament, I Kings 19:1-18.

Can you imagine a man of God, who had enough power with God, to shut heaven up for three years and six months? Can you imagine finding this man running for his life? Can you imagine finding this man saying, "Everybody's gone, Lord. They have killed everyone. They are after me and I have just had enough fit. I cannot take any more."

How close have you been to speaking like Elijah? Better yet, how many of you are there right now?

Physical causes. When you look at the physical causes of Elijah's discouragement; he was South of Beersheba, verse 3; in the wilderness, verse 4; under a Juniper tree verse 4 and Elijah was asking to die. He said, "Lord kill me; take my life."

Earlier, only 24 hours before this, Elijah had seen God's mighty power revealed. It is amazing and it never ceases to amaze me, God can heal your body today and can do a miraculous thing in your life today and tomorrow, there you are, somewhere crying and wondering will God do it again. If God did it once, God can do it again. That is settled.

Just twenty-four hours prior, God had revealed to Elijah up on Mt Carmel the mighty power of God. I Kings 18:1-17, 31, 34, 35, 36. He spoke out there like he was a man of God; Elijah walked out there and told the people to tear down all those altars that Ahab had built to worship Baal; I King 16:31; go get me twelve stones.

I Kings 18:31: dig some trenches around the sacrifice; four barrels of water and pour it on the burnt-sacrifice and on the wood. And he said do it the second time and he said do it the third time and they did it the third time verse 34; and the water ran 'round about the altar and he filled the trench also with water verse 35; soak it real good; then Elijah stood up and said, "God of Abraham, Isaac and Jacob, not for me, Lord, I do not need to be convinced. I know what you can do, Lord. But for all these that are standing around here, these unbelievers who are down here, Lord, if thou be God, answer by fire, verse 36.

And the Bible says, the fire fell down, licked up the water; burned up the Sacrifice, verse 38. Now here this same man is saying, "Lord, I have had enough, I cannot take any more.

Physical causes: Physical exhaustion and hunger are the two most common attacks that the devil can use to discourage us. Because you are human, many times, Elijah had gotten discouraged. Physical exhaustion can be very dangerous. At our weakest moments, the devil can attack you. From physical hunger the devil can attack you. We can find physical causes for discouragement, then there are times when you can find nothing but discouragement.

Spiritual Causes. There are some spiritual causes that you need to recognize. There are times when it seems it is impossible to find God anywhere. You look around and you say, "Lord, how can this be? Lord, I do not know what is going on. I am having difficulties. Jesus, it looks like there are only physical causes for my discouragement." This forces one to look at the spiritual causes.

When you lose your spiritual perspective, you want to die and you see everything wrong, especially, because you say, "Look, it wasn't that." There was no one looking for Elijah but Jezebel. You over react, lose your spiritual perspective and say things that you know are not right to say by a child of God and in relationship with God, should not say. You know God cares for you. You know God loves you. You know God has not abandon you. Why would you let the devil tell you that God does not care about you?

Can the devil lie? If nothing else, God awakened you. God has made ways for you and me. God has protected you on the highways and in the air. God has watched over you while we slept. God has healed your bodies. And the devil is going to tell you, God does not care about you and you are ready to die? This, my friend, is a trick of the devil. When you get in that condition, it is easy to say, "No one likes me. Everyone is against me."

When you hear people say that you should step back and look at them. Your mind should start working. How often do you go to church? When was the last time you attended a prayer meeting? When was the last time you attended a Bible class? Are you trying to live right? If you are doing all of these things, then the devil cannot discourage you. You know God said, "I will never leave you nor forsake you." Hebrew 13:5

If no one loves me, I know God loves me. If God be for us, who can be against us? Romans 8:31

God is more than the world against me. Why should I become upset becauseof my circumstances? If God is for me and I know God is for me, why should I worry? Why should I be in despair? Why should I be discouraged? There is no reason at all. No none whatsoever. Not only can you lose your physical causes and lose your spiritual perception, but you can lose your spiritual freshness. Can you picture Elijah on his knees praying for rain? Elijah is no longer spiritually fresh. Fear has replaced his faith. Spiritual freshness has become spiritually stagnated.

Here is a man who was down on his knees praying for God to bring rain and not only that, he could turn around and pray for God to stop the heavens from raining and all at once, this man who was so spiritually fresh, had lost all of that freshness and had become spiritually stagnant. Here he is, out there in the wilderness crying, running for his life, and saying nobody loves me. Saying, "... and I even I only, am left; and they seek my life, to take it away." I Kings 19:14

I am saying, if you are going to be a conqueror, you have got to learn how to conquer discouragement. You can find discouragement most places. It is everywhere. Not only must you look around and recognize the causes of discouragement but you must understand the consequences of discouragement. There are consequences of discouragement. If you will conquer discouragement, you must do more than recognize the causes. You must understand the consequences of discouragement.

The Bible says, Elijah meets Ahab: the prophet's challenge, I Kings 18:17-24:

Verse 17: *And it shall come to pass, that him that escapeth the sword of Hazael shall Jehu slay: and him that escapeth from the sword of Jehu shall Elisha slay.*

Verse 18: *Yet I have left me seven thousand in Israel, all the knees which have not bowed into Baal and every mouth which hath not kissed him.*

Verse 19: *Now therefore send, and gather to me all Israel unto mount Carmel, and the prophets of Baal four hundred and fifty, and the prophets of the groves four hundred, which eat at Jezebel's table.*

Verse 20: *So Ahab sent unto all the children of Israel, and gathered the prophets together unto mount Carmel.*

Verse 21: *And Elijah came unto all the people, and said, How long halt ye between two opinions? If the Lord be God, follow him: but if Baal, then follow him. And the people answered him not a word.*

Verse 22: *Then said Elijah unto the people, I, even I only, remain a prophet of the Lord; but Baal's prophets are four hundred and fifty men.*

Verse 23: *Let them therefore give us two bullocks; and let them choose one bullock for themselves, and cut it in pieces, and lay it on wood, and put no fire under: and I will dress the other bullock, and lay it on wood, and put no fire under.*

Verse 24: *And call ye on the name of your gods, and I will call on the name of the Lord: and the God that answereth by fire, let him be God. And all the people answered and said, It is well spoken.*

The Bible says, and the challenge was Jehovah versus Baal I Kings 18: 25–39

Verse 25: *And Elijah said unto the prophets of Baal, Choose you one bullock for yourselves, and dress it first;*

for ye are many; and call on the name of your gods, but put no fire under.*

Verse 26: *And they took the bullock which was given them, and they dressed it, and O Baal, hear us. But there was no voice, nor any that answered. And they leaped upon the altar which was made.*

Verse 27: *And it came to pass at noon, that Elijah mocked them, and said, Cry aloud; for he is a god; either he talking; or he is pursuing, or he is in a journey, or peradventure he sleepeth, and must be awaked.*

Verse 28: *And they cried aloud, and out themselves after their manner with knives and lancets, till the blood gushed out upon them.*

Verse 29: *And it came to pass, when midday was past, and they prophesied until the time of the offerings of the evening sacrifice, that there was neither voice, nor any to answer nor any that regarded.*

Verse 30: *And Elijah said unto all the people, Come near unto me. And all the people came near unto him. And he repaired the altar of the Lord that was broken down.*

Verse 31: *And Elijah took twelve stones, according to the number of the tribes of the sons of Jacob, unto whom the word of the Lord came, saying Israel shall be thy name:*

Verse 32: *And with the stones he built an altar in the name of the Lord: and he made a trench about the altar, as great as would contain two measures of seed.*

Verse 33: *And he put the wood in order, and cut the bullock in pieces, and laid him on the wood, and said, "Fill four barrels with water, and pour it on the burnt-sacrifice, and on the wood."*

Verse 34: *And he said, Do it the second time. And they did it the second time. And he said, Do it the third time. And they did it the third time.*

Verse 35: *And the water ran 'round about the altar; and he filed the trench also with water.*

Verse 36: *And it came to pass at the time of the offering of the evening sacrifice, that Elijah the prophet came near, and said, Lord God of Abraham, Isaac, and of Israel, let it be known this day that thou art God in Israel, and that I am thy servant, and that I have done all these things at thy word.*

Verse 37: *Hear me, O Lord, hear me, that this people may know that thou art the Lord God, and that thou hast turned their heart back again.*

Verse 38: *Then the fire of the Lord fell, and consumed the burnt-sacrifice and the wood, and the stones, and the dust, and licked up the water that was in the trench.*

Versed 39: *And when all the people saw it, they fell on their faces: and they said, The Lord, he is the God; the Lord, he is the God; the Lord, he is the God.*

Here we find the purpose of Israel. Israel was a nation headed back to God. A real revival was in the land. The people were crying, "The Lord, he is God. The Lord, he is God." Verse 39

But, look where God's man is; he is miles away under a Juniper Tree, crying, praying to God, "Lord take my life. Lord take my life. I want to die. They are after me". I Kings 19:4

The word of the Lord came to him and asked, "What doest thou here, Elijah? He answered "And he said, I have been very jealous for the Lord God of hosts: for the children of Israel have forsaken thy covenant, thrown down thine altars, and slain thy prophets with the sword; and I, even I only, am left; and thy seek my life, to take it away. Verse 10.

And a second time, there was a still small voice; vs 13, KJV; and there was a voice asking the question, "What doest thou here, Elijah?" And Elijah answered. And he said, I have been very jealous for the Lord God of hosts: because the children of Israel have forsaken thy covenant, thrown down thine altars, and slain thy prophets with the sword; and I even I only, am left and they seek my life, to take it away. Verse 14

Elijah was in the wilderness because of discouragement. Elijah felt forsaken. God had purpose for his life. You see, God has a purpose for you. There are many times. we feel that God has forsaken us. God has purpose for our lives. But God is working things out to get you in the right position before he can really bless you. You have got to be tried. You have to be proven. When you are ready, God will give you what he has for you. God is not just going to give you the desires of your heart until he knows you are able to handle it.

Negative thinking: 150 miles South of the place of victory. Oh yes, negative thinking. Discouragement can become a negative force. Consequently, Elijah visualizes himself as no better than his fathers. Can you imagine? The only true follower and he is the only one living for God. Everybody is gone but me, Lord. That is the way a lot of you sound. No one is living holy, but me. If you were living holy, you would see that someone else lives holy, too. If you are living holy, you could pray for others to live holy, too.

Negative thinking: Here in Elijah's writing, he wants to be killed and the words reveals the depths of his thoughts. Proverbs 23:7 says, "As a man thinketh in his heart, so is he:..." He was no better than anyone else. If you think you are a loser, you are a loser. If you think you are a winner, you are a winner. If you think everyone is against you, then everybody is against you. You think because you are thinking negatively, you are not going to be accepted. But you have got to ask God to help you. God will strengthen you. You cannot let the devil enter your thoughts. God loves me.

Conquering discouragement. You have got to accept the cure for discouragement. God will heal you of discouragement, but you have got to accept the cure for discouragement. Even in the midst of Elijah's discouragement, God was working, trying to get him to accept his cure for discouragement. God was working on Elijah. God allowed discouragement to come, but God always has an effective cure for discouragement. There is nothing you do that God does not have a cure. God has a cure for discouragement and it is effective. All God asked of us is to believe there is a cure for discouragement.

God cares for you. Look what God did for Elijah. Although Elijah's state of mind was not what God wanted it to be, God continued, tenderly reaching out to help his servant. When Elijah was down under the Juniper Tree, God gave him food, and God gave him water. God let Elijah rest a little while. God gave him shelter. All this was showing the wonderful evidence of God's love and care. Even though Elijah ran from God, and was in despair, and said, "Kill me; they are after me," but God let Elijah get to where he was going, and gave him a little rest, gave him some food, gave him some water, and gave him a place to stay.

Look what God is doing for you. You are crying and saying "God don't care for me." God has given you a job. God has healed your bodies. God has given you food to eat. God has given you a place to stay. God has given you clothes to wear. God has given you a car and you are crying and saying, "Lord, nobody loves me."

Just think, if God had gotten discouraged. What if God would get discouraged with those who have failed him, or what if God had gotten discouraged when we were not there when God needed us? What if God had gotten discouraged when we are not witnessing like we ought to be telling others about the saving grace of God?

You are living like you ought to be living and witnessing for God. God cannot depend on you because you are never there when God needs you, but yet and still God does not abdicate his obligation toward you. What God is going to do for you, he does it.

God provides companionship to help you, so God commanded Elijah, his private servant, to remain behind. God said, "You tell Elijah to stay back here; do not go now." But he could not escape the companionship of God.

The Division of Psalms 139:7-11:

Verse 7: *Wither shall I go or whither shall I flee from thy spirit? or whither shall I go from thy presence?*

Verse 8: *If I ascend up into heaven, thou art there: if I make my bed in hell, behold, thou are there.*

Verse 9: *If I take the wings of the morning, and dwell in the uttermost parts of the sea;*

Verse 10: *Even there shall thy hand lead me, and thy right hand shall hold me.*

Verse 11: *If I say, Surely the darkness shall cover me; even the night shall be light about me.*

Verse 12: *Yea, the darkness hideth not from thee; but the night shineth as the day: the darkness and the light are both alike to thee.*

Brothers and sisters, you ought to be glad God does not leave you when you get in the state of discouragement. Here is a man that felt terrible. He wanted to get away from the place where he was. Elijah wanted to hide himself until it was all over; just hid me somewhere Lord.

When God is walking with you, day and night look alike. There is no difference when God is there because God is light. He illuminates your way. You do not have to worry nor be discouraged. Do not worry about the darkness. Do not worry about being alone. Do not worry. God is with you. Do not let discouragement kill you. Do not let discouragement defeat you.

Yet I have left me seven thousand in Israel, all the knees which have not bowed unto Baal, and every mouth which hath not kissed him. I King 19:18

This is the victory that Elijah did not know. He thought he was the only one left and they were trying to kill him, but God had seven thousand in Israel who had not bowed to Baal. God knows more than we can think or ask. We have to believe God can remove discouragement and give us the victory. Remember God said, "I will never leave you nor forsake you. I am with you always."

Do not worry about what will happen. Do worry about what people will say. God is with you always. He will take care of you. Do not worry about friends. You can get the victory. Do not allow the devil to tell you God doesn't love you. God loves you. God loves all of you. God is on your side. There is nothing that can happen to you that God cannot handle. God can solve all your problems. The problems you may have, turn them over to Jesus. God can solve all your problems. You have the victory. If God be for you, who can be against you? If God is on your side you have the victory over discouragement.

You have determination. God put the crown of super conqueror on my head. I will not let anyone take my crown. I can conquer circumstances. I can conquer temptations. I can conquer fear and guilt. I can conquer worry and I can conquer discouragement.

SUPER CONQUERORS

Conquering Inconsistencies

Welcome to "Super Conquerors"
the fifth lesson of a six-part series.

St. Luke 22:31-34 — Jesus Predicts Peter's Denial
St. Luke 54-62 — Jesus arrested: Peter's denial

Our lesson is on Conquering Inconsistencies. Read St. Luke, Chapter 22:31-34 and 22:54-62

Read St. Luke 22:31-34:

Verse 31: *And the Lord said, Simon, Simon, behold, Satan hath desired to have you, that he may sift you as wheat:*

Verse 32: *But I have praye4d for thee, that thy faith fail not: and when thou art converted, strengthen thy brethren.*

Verse 33: *And he said unto him, Lord, I am ready to go with thee, both into prison, and to death.*

Verse 34: *And he said, I tell thee, Peter, the cock shall not crow this day, before that thou shalt thrice deny that thou knowest me.*

Read St. Louis 22:54-62:

Verse 54: *Then took they him, and led him, and brought him into the high priest's house. And Peter followed afar off.*

Verse 55: *And when they had kindled a fire in the midst of the hall, and were set down together, Peter sat down among them.*

Verse 56: *But a certain maid beheld him as he sat by the fire, and earnestly looked upon him, and said, This man was also with him.*

Verse 57: *And he denied him, saying Woman, I know him not.*

Verse 58: *And after a little while another saw him, and said, Thou art also of them. And Peter said, Man, I am not.*

Verse 59: *And about the space of one hour after another confidently affirmed, saying, Of a truth this fellow also was with him: for he is a Gallilean.*

Verse 60: *And Peter said, Man, I know not what thou sayest. And immediately, while he yet spake, the cock crew.*

Verse 61: *And the Lord turned, and looked upon Peter. And Peter remembered the word of the Lord, how he had said unto him, Before the cock crow, thou shalt deny me thrice.*

Verse 62: *And Peter went out, and wept bitterly.*

I request your attention to verse 61, "And the Lord turned, and looked upon Peter. And Peter remembered the word of the Lord, how he had said unto him, Before the cock crow, thou shall deny me thrice.

Our subject is Conquering Inconsistencies. Some of us may be in the same position Peter was in. Conquering inconsistencies is something people are not doing. The Bible has scriptures relative to people who are inconsistent.

Matthew 7:3: *And why beholdest thou the mote that is in thy brother's eye, but considerest not the beam that is in thine own eye?*

That is not consistent. That is inconsistent. You want to take the mote out of someone's eye and have a beam in your own eye. It does not make sense does it? But that is what happens. You are talking about someone else and you are doing the same thing they are doing. Paul shows us our inconsistencies in the scripture:

Romans 2:1 says,

THEREFORE *thou are inexcusable, O man, whosoever thou art that judgest: for wherein thou judgest another, thou condemnest thyself; for thou that judgest doest the same things.*

Inconsistency includes deceit, deception, hypocrisy, and falsehood. Inconsistency is not doing what you ought to be doing. As children of God, this is one of the things I am very much concerned about with each of you and that is that you have conquering attributes.

Does it disturb you the way some "saints of God" live their Christian lives? Aren't you disturbed by how "so-called Christians" live their Christian life? Everybody is a Christian but drinking. I was out this morning picking up some bottles. As I picked up a bottle one of the brothers said, "What is that in your hand, pastor?" It was an empty Old Grandad whisky bottle. I said, "I had better throw it away because someone will swear their pastor is drinking Old Grandad." That would be an example of judging. Some Christians do drink Grandad, don't they? They do that. So-called Christians do. Amen. They do that. But as saints of God, since your life has been changed, you don't do that.

It is really disturbing to see "saints of God" who are supposed to be Christians speaking, acting, and living life completely different from what you would expect from a child of God.

In fact, it is completely different from what the word of God would ask of you. Your testimony given and the life you live are inconsistent. It is impossible for people to see Christlikeness in people who are inconsistent. Your inconsistency is what keeps so many people from coming to church, from coming to Christ, and from getting saved. Many people are saying they are saved or that they are a Christian, but their actions do not validate what they say.

The drunk man on the corner says, "I'm a Christian and I go to reverend so and so's church." You cannot tell him he is not a Christian based on his lifestyle, and he will tell you there is nothing wrong with drinking.

Some Christians will tell you, there is nothing wrong with drinking as long as you don't get drunk. That is not consistent with God's word. There are many reasons used to excuse oneself from doing what is consistent with God's word. It seems inconsistency is the way of choice.

The so-called church members and the saints of God or Christians are no different than the rest of the non-church goers. If your testimony is inconsistent with the way you live, then this is plainly a life of inconsistency.

How consistent are you with what you testify? There are people who are not saved but try to act as if they are saved. That is not consistent. Being saved is a change from doing the things of the world to doing the things of God. If you are the devil, you cannot act like a saint of God on one occasion and the devil other times. You have got to act what you are. It is more disturbing the way you act and the way you live your life.

People talk about hypocrites knowing they are guilty, too. People talk about others and judge others, and we are doing the same things while we are judging other people.

You cannot see the mote in our eye for seeing the beam in another's eye. You cannot see inconsistency in ourselves, but you can see the inconsistency in the life of others.

While you can see the hypocrisy in the life of others, you must learn to conquer inconsistency in your life, otherwise you will not be the saint of God that God requires. God is requiring the saints of God to live Godly and to live what you testify.

You are guilty of inconsistencies, but you must conquer our inconsistencies. You are guilty, at times, of not understanding one another's problems or test or their trials. It should not be so difficult to understand one another; but sometimes it is hard to put ourselves in another person's position and try to understand what they are going through and harder to even have compassion.

You do not have compassion until it comes our time, then you say, "You don't understand; come on, you know what I am going through. It was a struggle to be here. It is a struggle to come to church today, and you don't know what others face when returning home." Think about the other persons who have unsaved or unchurched companions. Put yourself in their position and try to see the other side of that person's burden.

You must show your fellow saints some love when they are going through a test or a trial. You should be prepared to help them be victorious. You should be prepared to allow God to work in your life to help others. You must be conquerors.

In the lesson today, just as Peter had to learn to conquer his inconsistencies, you must learn to conquer our own inconsistencies. Many of you are inconsistent.

If everyone was consistent, there would be no problems at all. Tithe paying would not be a problem. Ministers would not have to quote Malachi 3:10: "Bring all the tithes into the storehouse, that there may be meat in mine house, and prove me now herewith, saith the Lord of hosts, if I will not open you the windows of heaven, and pour you out a blessing, that there shall not be room enough to receive it."

You need to take a lesson from Peter. Peter's life reveals some truth. Peter was one of the great disciples of our Lord and one that Jesus used all the time. The four gospels are full of information on Peter. Outside of the Lord's name, you find Peter's name all throughout the gospels. There is no other disciple's name used as much as Peter. No disciple spoke as much nor as often as Peter. Peter was the spokesperson. He did all the talking. Peter was not like the other disciples. There was something unique about Peter that was different from the other disciples. No other disciples were as inconsistent as Peter. Peter was not consistent.

You cannot condemn Peter. Peter's causes for inconsistencies were almost the same as yours. Your conduct is almost the same. Sometimes you can get a feeling of over confidence and that is what Peter felt. He had a sense of overconfidence. He put too much confidence in his own knowledge or flesh. This is a dangerous thing to do.

Peter felt above all the disciples, "Lord I am going to walk for you. Everyone can go, Lord, but I won't turn back. I am going to go with you, Lord."

Many of the causes of Peter's inconsistent conduct is the same as yours when you are over confident and thinking you are so great. Sometimes you get in that position and you seem to feel that you are the most important one.

Peter was supposed to be the most important disciple, because he was with Jesus all the time. His overconfidence in action and attitude was illustrated in Proverbs 16:28 "Pride goes before destruction and a haughty spirit before a fall."

You can see people who are swollen up with importance; thinking they are somebody great in the church; but all of you are sinners saved by grace. If it had not been for the grace of God, where would you be? If it had not been for the blood shed at Calvary where Jesus bought your salvation, where would you be? Stop and think about it. None of you would be here today if it had not been for the grace of God. God loved you.

The love of God bought you here today. If you are a sinner, God bought you to this church today. You did not just accidently come to this church. God drew you here today. God knew you needed to hear the truth. God knew you needed to be saved. You need to know that what you have been doing is not what God wants out of your life. Your life is not consistent with what God has written in the Bible.

All of you need to get your act together and don't think you are so confident that you become over-cocky and think that you have made it. The Bible says, "Pride goes before destruction and a haughty spirit before a fall." When you see people all swollen up with pride and are over-confident, it is not very long before the fall.

When God begins to bless you, you slow up. You cannot receive blessings with humility. You slow up. You had been faithful attending church, attending prayer meetings, attending Bible study, singing in the choir, and playing an instrument, now you don't show up. You want to do bigger and better positions, but you are unfaithful, and you want an unearned recognition.

You want to be seen. You may say, I don't just want to sing in the choir, I want to direct the choir. I don't want to play the piano; I want to play the organ because the organ players get more glory. Well, that is a bad attitude and it leads to a fall.

That kind of spirit will allow the devil to raise up and consume you. You will find yourself behind a mountain of inconsistencies. Your spirit will be blown up because no one realizes how important you are and no one thought about how important you are but you. You are the only one who thought you were important.

No one is important in God's program. It is God's program. You had better get yourself out of the way; change your attitude and line up with God's team and get on board without inconsistencies.

You need to say, "Lord, you can use me. God use me. If no one sees me or call my name, you can use me for your glory.

Brothers and sisters, you have got to learn how to conquer your inconsistencies.

It is true, pride goes before destruction and a haughty spirit before the fall. Peter though he was going to keep up until the pressure came. Someone said, "he's one of them." Then he said, "No, I am not one of them." The woman looked at him for about an hour. She even said, "You sound like him." "No."

One writer said, "He was cursing because he knew that saints don't curse. And he wanted to prove that he was not one of them. I am going to start cursing."

There are people who act like Peter. You do not want people to know you are one of them. You should be consistent. Do not let no one stop you from serving God. If you are a follower of Jesus Christ, live like you are a follower of Jesus Christ. If you are a member of a church, act like you are a member; if you are a visitor, say you are a visitorat that church. Do not act like you are a Christian and live like a sinner and say you are a member of a certain church. That is inconsistent. The lesson today is conquering inconsistencies.

Peter said, "I am loyal to you. I am going to be there." When the time came to prove his loyalty, he was not there. Peter thought he had matured in Christ but found he was not as mature as he thought he was. He denied Christ. He followed far behind him. He denied him three times. You must be strong spiritually to fight Satan. Satan has a bag of tricks he has not used yet and you have not seen yet.

Brothers and sisters, our strength comes from God. Do not be over-confident. Be loyal to God. Rely on God for your strength and for your growth in God as you mature. It is not by power, not by might, but by my spirit said the Lord. If you are going to be a conquer, you need the spirit of God working in your life. You need to understand that unless you have strong spiritual resources

The devil has years of fighting experience. The devil started off in deception and in hypocrisy. The story of Eve in the garden, Genesis Chapter 3. Eve had been going around talking to the Lord every day, consistently, until one day Adam and Eve was not there. The Lord went looking for them. They had been there all the time, now he could not find them. "Adam, Where art thou?"

Brothers and sisters, you have got to learn how to conquer inconsistencies. You have got to face the devil with the resources of God; not on your own strength. You have got to use God's word. Nothing frightens the devil more than the word of God and the resource of prayer and dedication.

You are a conqueror of Circumstances, a Conqueror of Temptations, a Conqueror of Fear, a Conqueror of Discouragement and a Conqueror of Inconsistencies.

SUPER CONQUERORS

Conquering Worry

Welcome to "Super Conquerors"
the sixth lesson of a six-part series.

The Epistle of Paul the Apostle to the Philippians
The divisions are indicated by the Chapters:

I.   *Christ, the believer's Life, rejoicing in suffering, Chapter l:1-30;*

II.   *Christ, the believer's pattern, rejoicing in lowly service, Chapter 2:1-30;*

III.   *Christ, the believer's object, rejoicing despite imperfections, Chapter 3:1-21;*

IV.   *Christ, the believer's strength, rejoicing over anxiety, 5:1-23*

Philippians 4:5–9
The secret of the peace of God

Verse 5: *Let your moderation be known unto all men. The Lord is at hand.*

Verse 6: *Be careful for nothing; but in everything by prayer and supplication with thanksgiving let your request be made known unto God.*

Verse 7: *And the peace of God, which passeth all understanding shall keep your hearts and minds, through Christ Jesus.*

The presence of the God of peace

Verse 8: *Finally, brethren, whatsoever things are true, whatsoever things are honest, whatsoever things are just, whatsoever things are pure, whatsoever things are of good report; if there be any virtue, and if there be any praise, think on these things.*

Verse 9: *Those things, which ye have both learned, and received, and heard, and seen in me, do; and the God of peace shall be with you. The opposite of peace is worry.*

Our lesson is on Conquering Worry. Before we can claim to be super conquerors, we will have to conquer worry. The question that comes to mind is "How devastating is worry?"

Conquering Worry. Some of you are worried about aches and pains. Some of you have bills, some of you worry about your car being old and falling apart, some of you worry about your unruly children, and some of you worry about your companion that is unfaithful. Most of us is worried about something.

Some people will say, "I am not worried." Some people will say, "I'm just concerned." Even if you put it under different heading, it is worry.

Doctors tell you that many of the problems plaguing the human race, or modern man, are directly related to worry. Most of your sicknesses comes from worry and stress. When you start worrying, your blood pressure will go up. When you start worrying, your stomach gets upset. When you start worrying, you have sleepless nights.

People worry if their aches and pains could be a sign of cancer. Well, every ache or pain is not cancerous. God can heal cancer, yet we worry.

It has been said that worry is now known as public enemy number one.

Seemingly, worry knows no boundaries from the standpoint of cultural or financial backgrounds. All cultures can suffer from worry whether rich or poor. The rich worry about how they are going to save money while the poor worry about their next welfare check.

There is no category that cannot be associated with worry. Cultural, social, economic backgrounds have nothing to do with whether you worry or not. All people worry.

The synonym for worry is concern, apprehension, fear, care, burden, uneasiness, disquiet, discomfort, unease, nervousness, fret, agonize, stew, fuss, be anxious, troubled, lose sleep, bothered, pester.

The Bible does not speak to all of the synonyms, but it does speak to the following:

1. **Apprehension:** Philippians 3:12 Not as though I had already attained, either were already perfect: but I follow after, if that I may apprehend that for which also, I am apprehended of Christ Jesus.

   Act 12:4: *And when he had apprehended him, he put him in prison, and delivered him to four quaternions of soldiers to keep him; intending after Easter to bring him forth to the people.*

2. **Fear:** Job 28:28: And unto man he said, Behold, the fear of the Lord, that is wisdom; and to depart from evil is understanding.

   Ps 2:11: *Serve the Lord with fear and rejoice with trembling.*

3. Care:

I Peter 5:7 *Casting all your care upon him; for he careth for you.*

4. Fret:

Ps 37:1 *Fret not thyself because of evildoers, neither be thou envious against the workers of iniquity.*

The word, "worry" does not appear in the King James translation of the Bible. The word that has much of the same meaning as worry, in the Greek, would be "divided mind." When you are worried, you have a divided mind. The book of James 1:8 says, "A double minded man is unstable in all his ways." A man with a divided mind. Some of you have a divided mind. Many of you are worried about what is going to happen tomorrow and tomorrow has not even come. We may be a corpse by tomorrow, but you are worrying about tomorrow. There may be some things you may have to face tomorrow that you may not want to face, consequently, you are worried.

School children worry about examinations or about the paper that is due and not completed. If something happed on your job Friday, you may not want to face your boss on Monday. Worry is what we do, it is what happens when we do not have control over any given situation.

These timely words written by Paul to the saints at Philippi gives us the advice needed to conquer worry. Paul gave us the remedy to conquer worry. No one has to accept worry. Paul said, "Rejoice in the Lord always, and again I say rejoice. (Philippians 3:1)

But, Paul, "What about worry?" Paul would say, "Rejoice." That is something, isn't it?

Most of you would say, that was in Paul's day; he does not know anything about the twenty-first century. He does not know what you are going through. He does not know about the troubles you have. It was easy for Paul to say that in his day, "rejoice." He did not have television. He didn't have the problems you are having. Therefore, Paul, does not know what you are going through.

You may further say, in Paul's time, it was very easy to be a saint, but it is hard to be saved today. The devil just stays on you all the time; It looks like everywhere you turn, there is trouble and Paul said, "Rejoice."

You may ask, how can you rejoice when people mistreat you? How can you rejoice when people talk against you? How can you rejoice when your body is racked with pain? How can you rejoice if you do not know where your next meal will come? But Paul says, "Rejoice."

Paul is a conqueror? Paul is right. I know Paul is right. What makes me know Paul is right is because Paul penned these words from the Roman prison. It an indication that Paul was conquering worry. He was in prison telling others to "rejoice always, and again I say rejoice."

The Bible shows us, Paul was conquering worry. Paul conquered worry by being glad. You can conquer worry be being glad, by rejoicing and thanking God that whatever happens to you, it could have been worse. It could have been worse than what it was. If you lost one arm, you could have lost two arms. Thank God, he saved one arm. If you do not get three meals, thank God you got one meal. Be glad.

By being glad, you gain the victory. You say, be glad about what? Be glad for what God has done for you. Paul had every human reason to be upset. He had reasons to be filled with worry. As God's missionary, as God's evangelist, as God's man, he was isolated in a dungeon. Here is a man, namely Jesus Christ, that Paul had fallen in love with; Paul; had gone on missionary journeys; had preached the gospel of Jesus Christ; had been telling everybody about the power of God and what God could do, and yet he was locked up in prison and Paul is saying, "rejoice."

You cannot find where Paul was worried about when he was going to get out of prison; nor what he was going to eat. Paul was not worried about who was going to come and visit him. Paul was not worried about any one sending him a letter; no one calling him. Paul did not preach to a large crowd in prison. No one was coming to hear the great Apostle Paul. He was isolated. Nobody was able to hear him. When you preach you want everyone to hear you, but not so for Paul, he had no one to listen to him in the prison.

Paul could not visit the churches he loved. Even under those most trying conditions, under those grave circumstances, Paul was conquering worry. You do not find Paul worrying at all. He conquered worry by being glad for what the Lord had done for him.

When you find yourselves in trouble, instead of worrying about things which you cannot change, thank God for what he had done for you. You cannot change the weather; you cannot change snow; cannot change rain; only God can do that. Change does not happen by wishing you could make a change, but God can change things through prayers.

Why should you worry over circumstances you have no control; thank God you are still here; thank God for what he has done for you; thank God he has loved you;

thank God he has protected you; and thank God he has cared for you.

You are one of God's chosen vessels. You are one of God's private possessions. God is not going to let anything happen to his private property. God has his name on you and God is saying to Satan, "keep your hands off my private property; you are fragile; do not handle too rough."

God saved you. Why should you worry when you know God loves you? Why should you worry when you know God protects you? Why should you worry when you know God cares for you?

Not only did God save you, but God keeps you, not against your will but you are glad for what God had done in your life.

Paul had confidence in the goodness of God based on what God had done in his life. You see, brothers and sisters, you have got to know what God will do. Paul knew that worrying would not make any valuable change in his life. Worrying is not going to make any valuable change in your life, so why worry?

If you have Christ as your Lord and great God, if you have Christ as your Savior, you can be assured that God is working in your life for your good.

Often, what you are worrying about, God has worked it out. You do not have to worry about God, because he will perform. God is working on your behalf. God is working while you are worrying about your problems.

Paul wrote, Ephesians 2:10:

Verse 10: *For we are his workmanship, created in Christ Jesus unto good works, which God hath before ordained that we should walk in them.*

God has already worked things out for your life. God has already ordained how you should walk and you are worried about what direction you should go and what is down the road. Do not worry about what is down the road. Do not worry because the Lord knows the way that you take.

Job 23:10 says:

Verse 10: *But he knoweth the way that I take: when he hath tried me, I shall come forth as gold.*

God will always be with you. In the book of Hebrew 13:5:

Verse 5: *Let your conversation be without covetousness and be content with such things as ye have: for he hath said, I will never leave thee, nor forsake thee.*

God has said, "I will never leave thee nor forsake thee. God will always be with you. God wants his best for you. Sometimes, you accept second best, butGod has better things for you. He has something better for you, but you get impatient. You do not wait on what God has for you. God only gives good gifts to his people.

The Bible says, Division of Psalms 37:4:

Verse 4: *Delight thyself also in the Lord; and he shall give thee the desires of thine heart.*

God will always give you good gifts. God will always be with you. Paul says in Romans 8:35:

Verse 35: *Who can separate us from the love of Christ? Shall tribulation, or distress, or persecution, or famine, or nakedness, or peril, or sword?*

And, brothers and sisters, I am saying, who shall separate you from the Love of God? Do not let nothing stop you from loving God. God will always love you even if you turn away from God. God still loves you.

The parable of the lost son, in Luke 15:11 – 24:

Verse 11: *And he said, A certain man had two sons:*

(The departure)

Verse 12: *The younger of them said to his father, Father, give me the portion of goods that faileth to me. And he divided unto them his living.*

Verse 13: *And not many days after the younger son gathered all together, and took his journey into a far country, and there wasted his substance with riotous living.*

(The misery of the far country.)

Verse 14: *And when he had spent all, there arose a mighty famine in that land; and he began to be in want.*

Verse 15: *And he went and joined himself to a citizen of that country; and he sent him into his fields to feed swine.*

Verse 16: *And he would fain have filled his belly with the husks that the swine did eat: and no man gave unto him.*

(The repentance)

Verse 17: *And when he came to himself, he said, How many hired servants of my father's have bread enough and to spare, and I perish with hunger!*

Verse 18: *I will arise and go to my father, and will say unto him, Father, I have sinned against heaven, and before thee.*

Verse 19: *And am no more worthy to be called thy son: make me as one of thy hired servants.*

(The return and the father.)

Verse 20: *And he arose, and came to his father. But when he was yet a great way off, his father saw him, and had compassion, and ran, and fell on his neck, and kissed him.*

Verse 21: *And the son said unto him, Father, I have sinned against heaven, and in thy sight, and am no more worthy to be called thy son.*

Verse 22: *But the father said to his servants, Bring forth the best robe, and put it on him; and put a ring on his hand, and shoes on his feet:*

(The rejoicing.)

Verse 23: *And bring hither the fatted calf, and kill it; and let us eat, and be merry:*

Verse 24: *For this my son was dead, and is alive again; he was lost, and is found. And they began to be merry.*

God is waiting to say, "Come Home." He is waiting to put the robe on you. God is waiting to put the ring on your finger. God is waiting to put shoes on your feet. God is waiting to kill the fatted calf. God is waiting on you to make up your mind to come back home.

I am talking about conquering worry. There is no need to worry. Why should you worry when God is very much concerned about you? God is the God of what he wills.

You waste a lot of time worrying about situations that you cannot change and when all you have to do is take it to Jesus in prayer and turn it over to the Lord. One song writer wrote, "Take your burdens to the Lord and leave them there." Do not wrestle with your problems, do not struggle with your problems, just say, "Lord, here are my problems."

Do what Hezekiah did, when Hezekiah got the letter that the Assyrians army, he did not get upset. It was frightening because everybody was saying, "What are we going to do?" The Assyrian army was a great army.

But Hezekiah went into the sanctuary and he said, "Look Lord, you read what he wrote. You know what Hezekiah said, and it is true, too. Hezekiah said, he had conquered nations, he had torn down their gods, who were not God, but were made by men's hands. Hezekiah went in and tore gods down and burned them up. Hezekiah said, "But look, you read the letter. It is your problem."

2 Chronicles 31:1, 7, 8:

Verse 1: *Now when all this was finished all Israel that were present went out to the cities of Judah, and brake the images in pieces, and threw down the high places and the altars out of all Judah and Benjamin, in Ephraim also and Manasseh, until they had utterly destroyed them all. Then all the children of Israel returned every man to his possession, into their own cities.*

Verse 7: *Be strong and courageous, be not afraid nor dismayed for the king of Assyria, nor for all the multitude that is with him: for there be more with us than with him;*

Verse 8: *With him is an arm of flesh; but with us is the LORD our God to help us, and to fight our battles. And the people rested themselves upon the words of Hezekiah king of Judah.*

Sennacherib seeks to terrify the inhabitants of Jerusalem (II King 18:17-25)

2 Chronicles 32:9,16:

Verse 9: *After this did Sennacherib king of Assyria send his servants to Jerusalem, (but he himself laid siege against*

Lachish, and all his power with him,) unto all his power with him,) unto Hezekiah king of Judah, and unto all Judah that were at Jerusalem, saying

Verse 16: *I And his servants spake yet more against the LORD God, and against his servant Hezekiah.*

Sennacherib defies the God of Hezekiah (II Kings 19:9-13)

2 Chronicles 32:17-19:

Verse 17: *He wrote also letters to rail on the LORD God of Israel, and to speak against him, saying, As the gods of the nations of other lands have no delivered their people out of mine hand, so shall not the God of Hezekiah deliver his people out of mine hand.*

Verse 18: *Then they cried with a loud voice in the Jews' speech unto the people of Jerusalem that were on the wall, to affright them, and it trouble them; that they might take the city.*

Verse 19: *And they spake against the God of Jerusalem, as against the gods of the people of the earth which were the work of the hands of man.*

Hezekiah' s prayer (II King 19:14-19) Jehovah destroys the Assyrian army (II King 19:3536)

2 Chronicles 32:21:

Verse 21: *And the LORD sent an angel, which cut off all the mighty men of valour, and the leaders and captains in the camp of the king of Assyria. So he returned with the shame of face to his own land. And when he was come into the house of his god, they that came forth of his own bowels slew him there with the sword.*

Brothers and sisters, I do not see where Hezekiah worried at all. I do not see where Hezekiah was watching to see where the army was positioned. I do not see where Hezekiah asked, "How close are they to getting me?"

The angel of the Lord fought Hezekiah's battle. God took care of the problem. Hezekiah got the victory.

Brothers and sisters, you see, God can fight your battle, no matter what the problems. Don't worry about things when God can take care of them. Why get out of the will of God trying to fight your own battles when God can fight for you? Do not worry. You cannot praise God and worry at the same time. You do not pray and worry at the same time. If you are going to worry, don't pray and if you are going to pray, don't worry.

Do worry about what people are doing or saying. Do not worry about how things look. Do not worry. Be glad for what God can do for you. You have this assurance that God want the best for you. You can be confident that the very thing God has begun in you, that good work, he will perform it until the day of Jesus Christ.

Philippian 1:6:

Verse 6: *Being confident of this very thing, that he which hath begun a good work in you will perform it until the day of Jesus Christ:*

Nothing will stop God from working on you to make you what he wants you to become. It is your faith that will help you become your best.

If you have a problem, talk to God. Tell God about your problems not everyone, but God. Worry and prayer do not go together. If you pray, don't worry. If you do not pray, you have worry. Prayer is not a game. Paul said, "In everything by prayer and supplication with thanksgiving, let your request be made known unto God."

(The secret of the peace of God.)

Philippians 4:6

Verse 6: *Be careful for nothing; but in every thing by prayer and supplication with thanksgiving let your requests be made known unto God.*

Verse 7: *And the peace of God, which passeth all understanding, shall keep your hearts and minds through Christ Jesus.*

If your prayer is to be effective, then your prayer must be honest. Tell God what you are feeling. If you are scared, you tell the Lord, you are scared and if you are fearful, you tell God you are fearful. You tell God you need more faith to stand on his word. Lord, only you can fight my battle. Lord help me hold my peace and let you fight my battle.

I am talking about conquering worry. Everyone is worried about something. You have got to be honest. Talk honest with God. Tell God your needs. Tell God your desires. Tell God you want victory. You need to conquer worry.

As your leader, I am not going to waste my good days in front of me worrying *about* what is going to happen if I die. I am admonishing you, do some "thankful talking" to the Lord. Get on your knees and tell God how much you thank him. Tell God thank you for the victory. Thank you, Lord for what you are doing for me.

Over and over, the Bible teaches that saints are to be thankful in their prayers. Simply counting our blessings and count them one by one.

The Division of Psalms 103:1-5:

Verse 1: *Bless the Lord, O my soul: and all that is within me, bless his holy name.*

Verse 2: *Bless the Lord, O my soul and forget not all his benefits:*

Verse 3: *Who forgiveth all thine inquities; who health all thy diseases;*

Verse 4: *Who redeemeth thy life from destruction; who crowneth thee with lovingkindness and tender mercies;*

Verse 5: *Who satisfieth thy mouth with good things; so that thy youth is renewed like the eagle's.*

Do not worry. Count your blessings. What did the Lord do for David? The Lord who healeth us from all diseases; redeemeth us from destruction, who satisfies your mouth with good things. A song writer wrote, count your blessings; name them one by one; when you have finished, you will be surprised at what the Lord has done.

Sometimes you need to get on your knees and thank God movement of your hands, feet; some people cannot move their hands and some people cannot move their feet. Some people only have one foot. You can thank God for two feet. You can thank God for eyes to see. Thank God for reasonable portion of health. If you thank God for those things, you will find out you won't worry too much. Thank God for everything in your life. Thank God you can trust him. You can conquer worry by thanking God.

Paul was painfully aware that worry could never be conquered until your thought processes change. The bible says in Proverbs 23:7:

Verse 7a: *"For as he thinketh in his heart so is he..."*

Paul wrote in Philippians 4:8:

Verse 8: *Finally brethren, whatsoever things are true, whatsoever things are honest, whatsoever things are just, whatsoever things are pure, whatsoever things are lovely, and whatsoever things are of a good report; if there be any virtue, and if there be any praise, think on these things.*

Thank God for the privilege of prayer. Thank God for the privilege of entering the house of prayer. In some countries, people have to slip and pray. In America you have the privilege to pray freely.

The Lord knows how to send catastrophes and tragedies to get you to pray. When the tragedy happened with the space shuttle, the president asked all America to pray. Prayer had been taken out of the schools; but on that day, all Americans were asked to pray. When God wants prayer, God knows how to get prayer. When the space shuttle blew up, prayer was in the school, in Congress and even the president was praying.

You need to praise God while you have a chance. You need to praise God now. Praise God in the sanctuary. Praise God you have the victory over worrying.

In all these six areas of your life, as you walk with God, you are a super conqueror. You have the tools to conquer circumstances; conquer temptations; conquer fear; conquer discouragement; conquer inconsistencies and conquer worry.

About the Author

The author, Thelma Manning Hall, was privileged to work with Bishop Charles Edward Davis for more than sixty-five years of his ninety-six years.

When he served as youth president, president of the choir, financial chairman, at the request of his wife, Geraldine Olivia Davis, the author worked with him as secretary, and administrative assistant on his spiritual journey at the Indiana Avenue Pentecostal Church of God, Inc.,

When Bishop Charles Edward Davis served as Convention Committee Coordinator and Convention Committee Chairman for the Pentecostal Assemblies of the World, Inc, she served as his executive administrative assistant for ten years.

The author had many creative tasks assigned to her and it perfected her skills to attain higher professional levels. The author's motivation was inspired by Bishop Charles Edward Davis, who accepted nothing less than perfection and encouraged her to reach higher for excellence on each task assigned.

She succeeded. To date, Thelma Manning Hall has achieved and completed, with honors, elementary, high school, college and graduate degrees. The poem, by Robert Ricciardelli, depicts the complete story of the author's perseverance, determination and faith in God.

The Road to Success

The road to SUCCESS IS NOT STRAIGHT
There is a CURVE called failure.
A LOOP called CONFUSION.
SPEED BUMPS called FRIENDS.
RED LIGHTS called ENEMIES.
CAUTION LIGHTS called FAMILY.
You will have FLATS called JOBS
But, if you have a SPARE called DETERMINATION.
An ENGINE called PERSEVERANCE.
INSURANCE called FAITH.
A DRIVER called JESUS.
YOU WILL MAKE IT TO A PLACE
Called S – U – C – C – E – S – S!!